T0022506

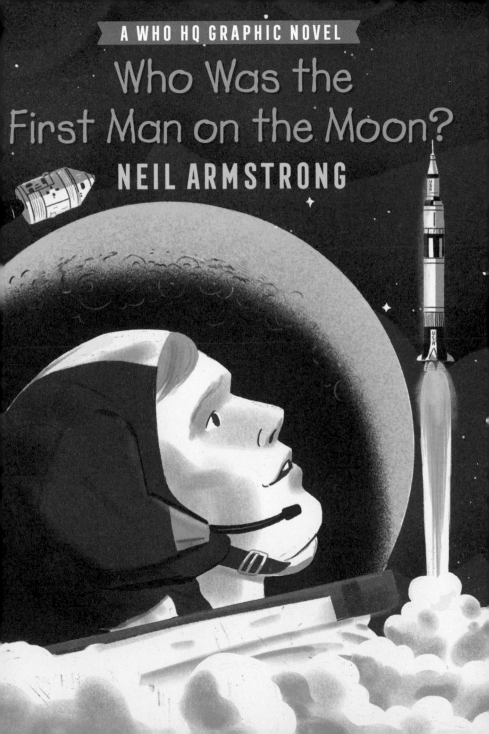

For Cameron and Hayden—NP

In loving memory of Shirley Dennis.
Thank you, Grandma—DS

PENGUIN WORKSHOP
An Imprint of Penguin Random House LLC, New York

Penguin supports copyright. Copyright fuels creativity, encourages diverse voices, promotes free speech, and creates a vibrant culture. Thank you for buying an authorized edition of this book and for complying with copyright laws by not reproducing, scanning, or distributing any part of it in any form without permission. You are supporting writers and allowing Penguin to continue to publish books for every reader.

The publisher does not have any control over and does not assume any responsibility for author or third-party websites or their content.

Copyright © 2021 by Penguin Random House LLC. All rights reserved.
Published by Penguin Workshop, an imprint of Penguin Random House LLC, New York.
PENGUIN and PENGUIN WORKSHOP are trademarks of Penguin Books Ltd.
WHO HQ & Design is a registered trademark of Penguin Random House LLC.
Manufactured in China.

Image on TV on page 56 courtesy NASA

Visit us online at www.penguinrandomhouse.com.

Library of Congress Cataloging-in-Publication Data is available upon request.

ISBN 9780593224434 (pbk)   10 9 8 7 6 5 4 3 2 1 HH
ISBN 9780593224441 (hc)   10 9 8 7 6 5 4 3 2 1 HH

Lettering by Comicraft
Book design by Jay Emmanuel

This is a work of nonfiction. All of the events that unfold in the narrative are rooted in historical fact. Some dialogue and characters have been fictionalized in order to illustrate or teach a historical point.

For more information about your favorite historical figures, places, and events, please visit www.whohq.com.

A WHO HQ GRAPHIC NOVEL

Who Was the First Man on the Moon?

NEIL ARMSTRONG

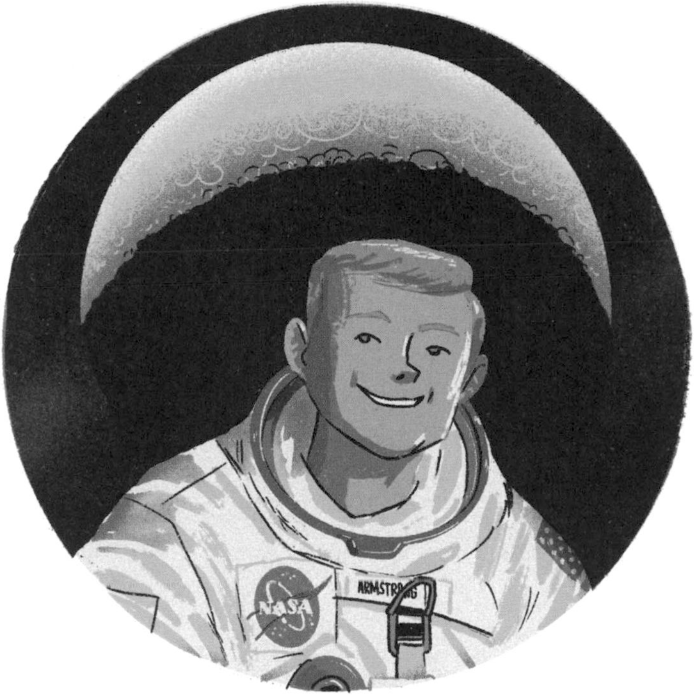
NASA
ARMSTRONG

by Nathan Page
illustrated by Drew Shannon

Penguin Workshop

Introduction

Neil Armstrong was born August 5, 1930, on the edge of a small farming town called Wapakoneta, Ohio, where the land is flat and on a clear day the skies are limitless.

Neil loved reading, building model planes, and looking after his younger siblings. He experimented a lot as a boy, tinkering, exploring, and always wanting to learn more about the world around him. Sometimes Neil's experiments were outright disasters. But with each disaster, he became more familiar with risk and when it was a good time to take one.

His curiosity with the world continued throughout his life. He learned how to fly planes when he was still in high school, served as a Navy pilot during the Korean War, and then graduated from college as an aeronautical engineer. He was a pilot of experimental planes like the X-15, and because of his reputation for being able

to fly any aircraft, in 1962, NASA selected him to be among their second group of astronauts.

On July 16, 1969, Neil set out on a spaceflight with his fellow crew members, Buzz Aldrin and Michael Collins, at the Kennedy Space Center in Cape Canaveral, Florida. All systems were go: The crew at the NASA Mission Control Center located in Houston, Texas, was ready for liftoff, and the entire world was watching. Neil had no idea how this experiment would unfold—all he knew was that he wasn't in Wapakoneta anymore. And this time, there was no room for mistakes.

Every experiment, every takeoff and landing, all the falls and moments too close to call, got Neil to July 20, 1969: the day he became the first man to walk on the moon.

This was known as the Apollo 11 mission.

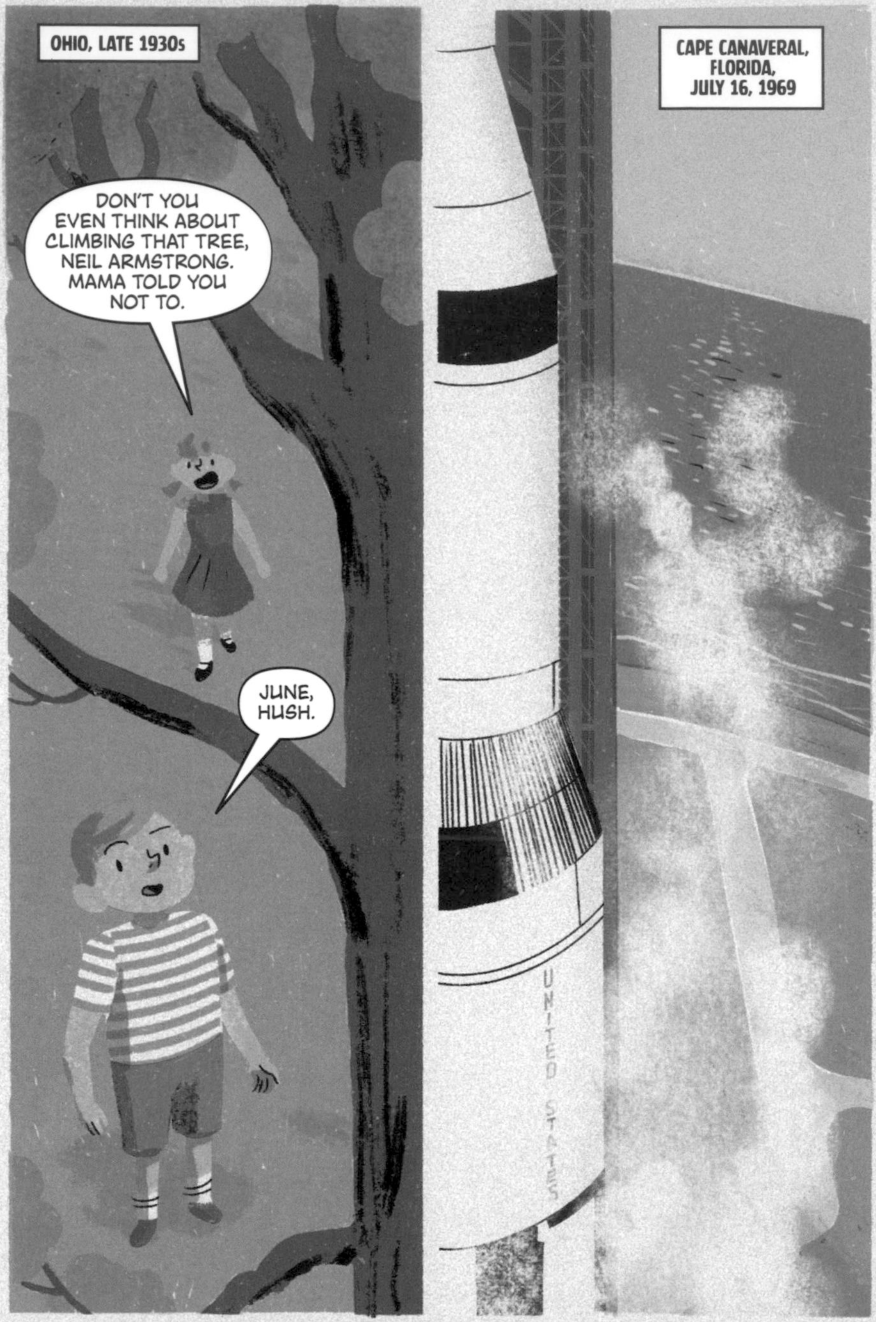
OHIO, LATE 1930s
DON'T YOU EVEN THINK ABOUT CLIMBING THAT TREE, NEIL ARMSTRONG. MAMA TOLD YOU NOT TO.
JUNE, HUSH.
CAPE CANAVERAL, FLORIDA, JULY 16, 1969
UNITED STATES

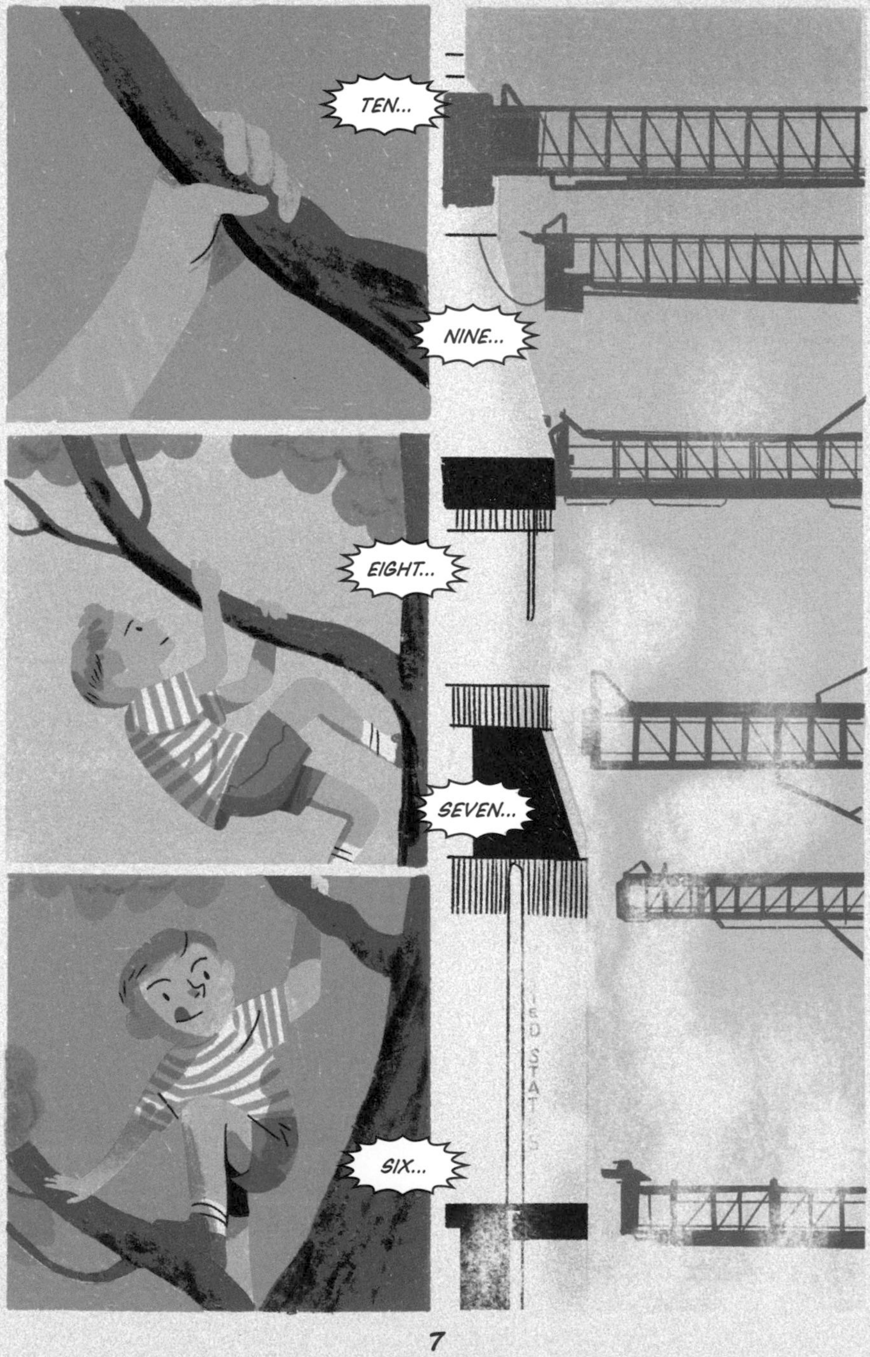
TEN...
NINE...
EIGHT...
SEVEN...
SIX...

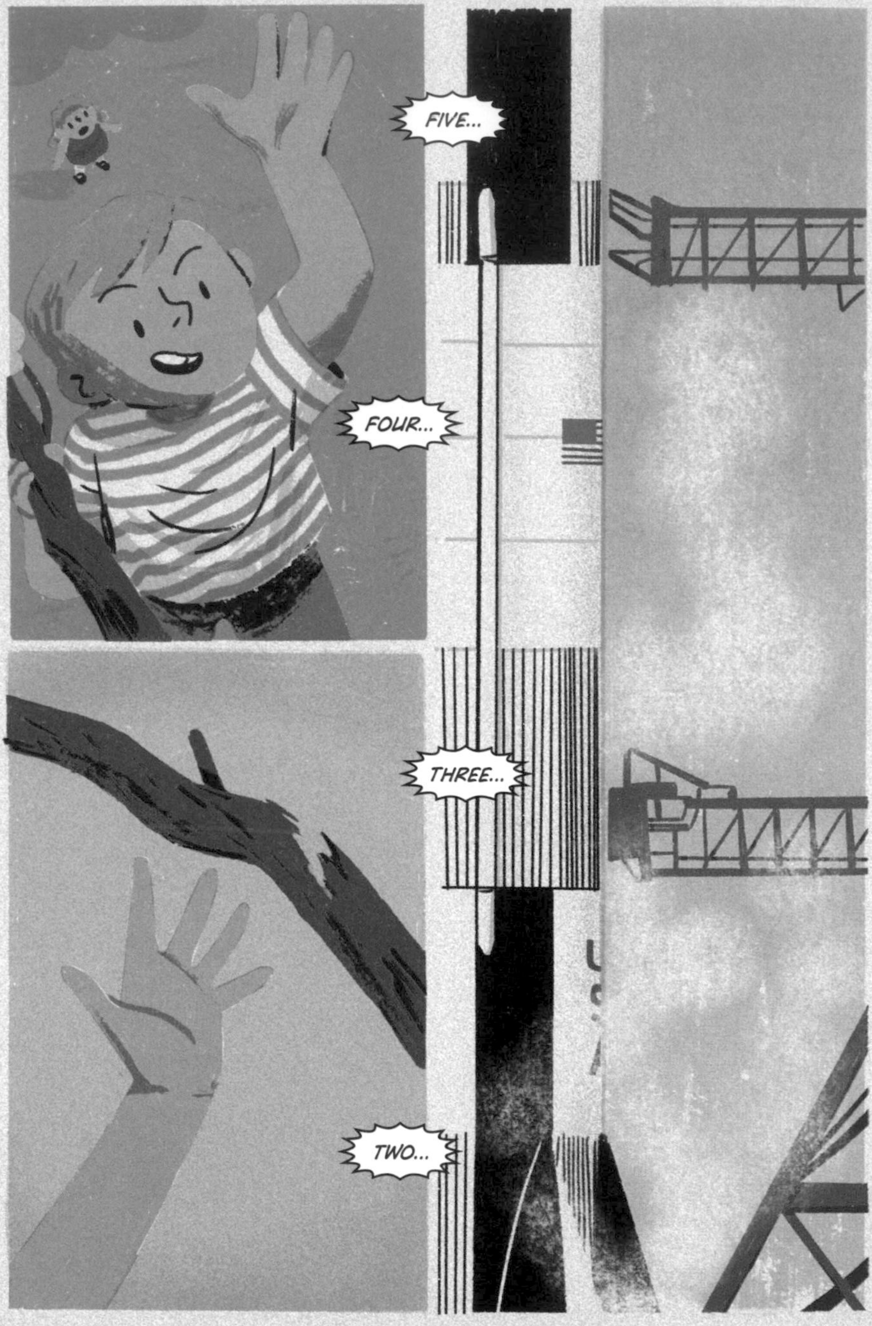
FIVE...
FOUR...
THREE...
TWO...

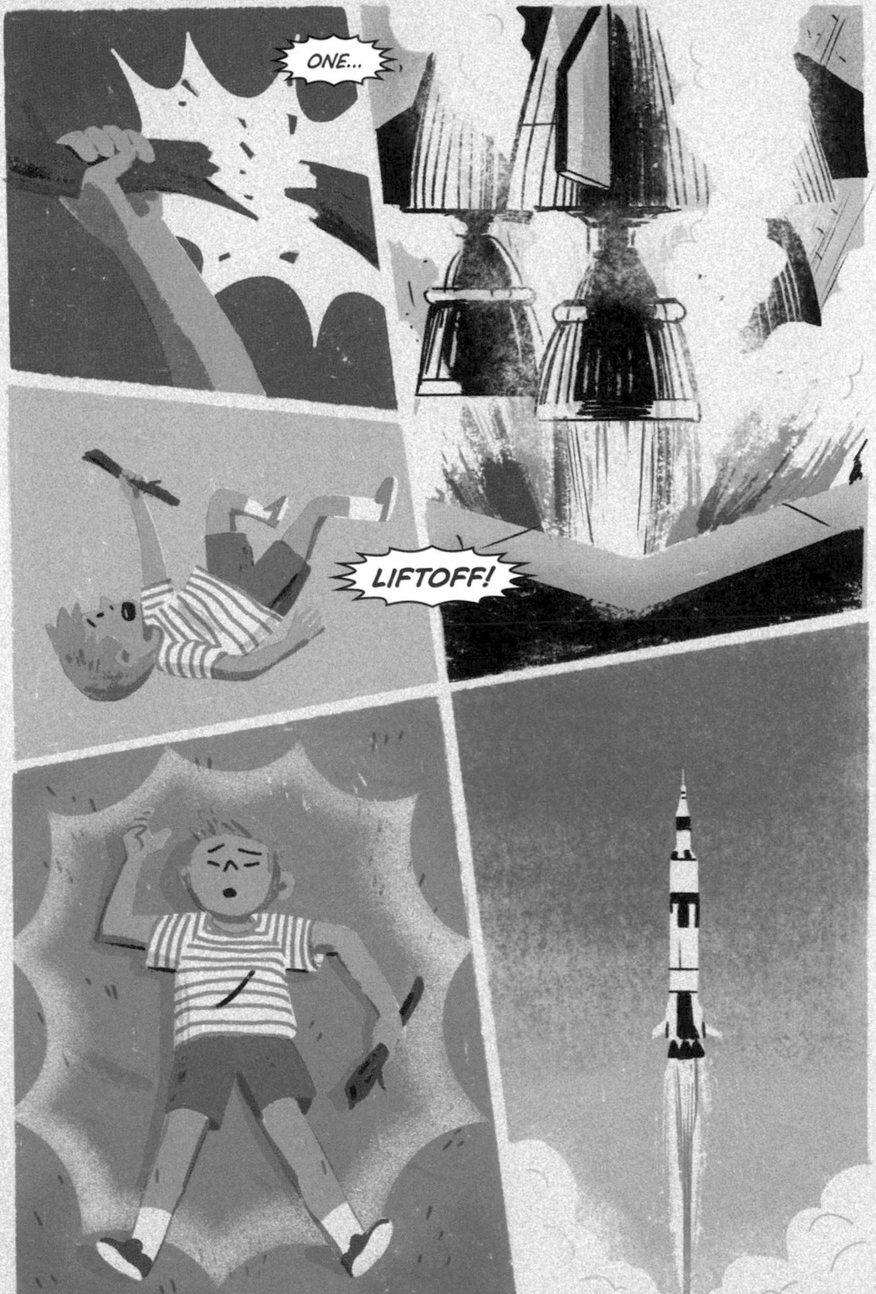
ONE...
LIFTOFF!

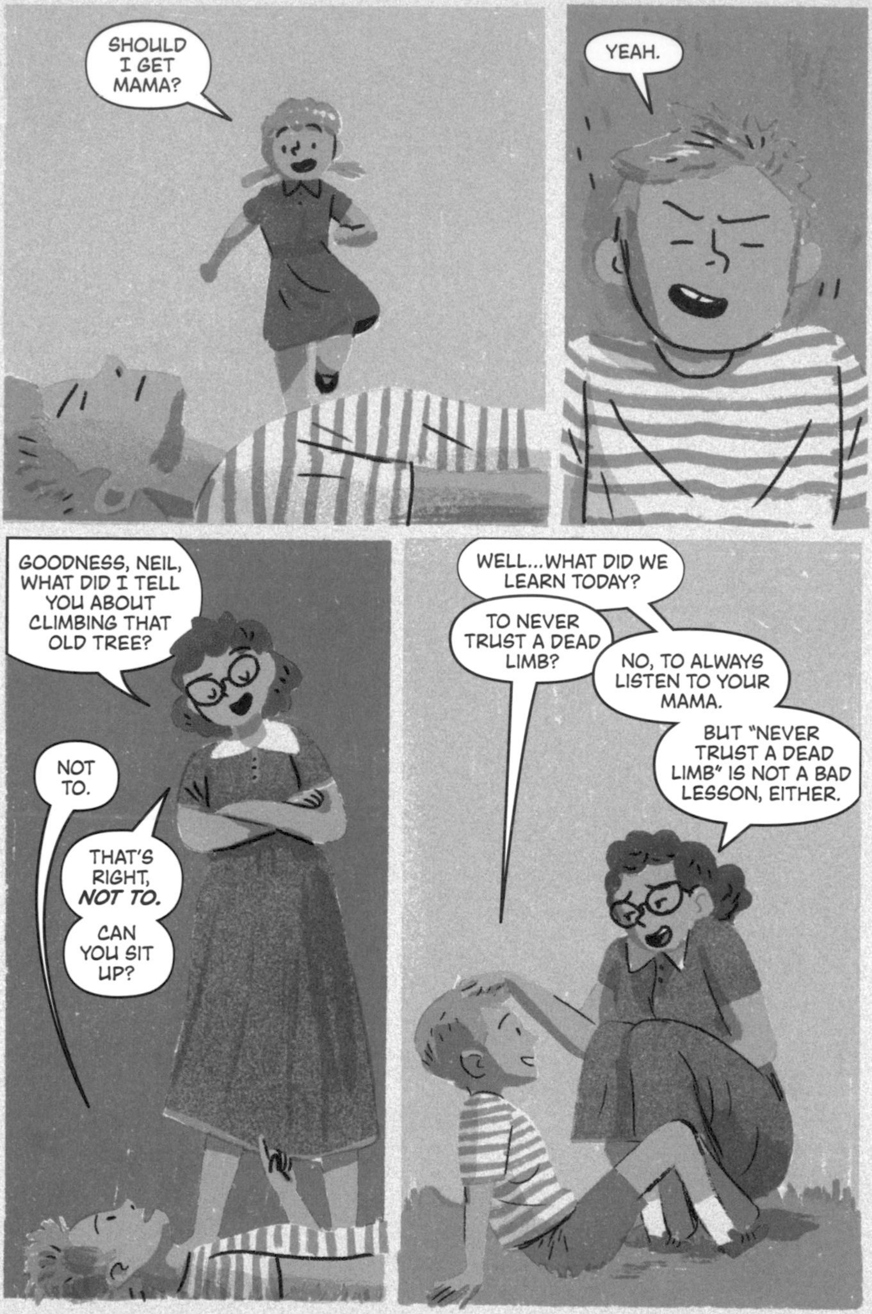
SHOULD I GET MAMA?
YEAH.
GOODNESS, NEIL, WHAT DID I TELL YOU ABOUT CLIMBING THAT OLD TREE?
NOT TO.
THAT'S RIGHT, *NOT TO.*
CAN YOU SIT UP?
WELL...WHAT DID WE LEARN TODAY?
TO NEVER TRUST A DEAD LIMB?
NO, TO ALWAYS LISTEN TO YOUR MAMA.
BUT "NEVER TRUST A DEAD LIMB" IS NOT A BAD LESSON, EITHER.

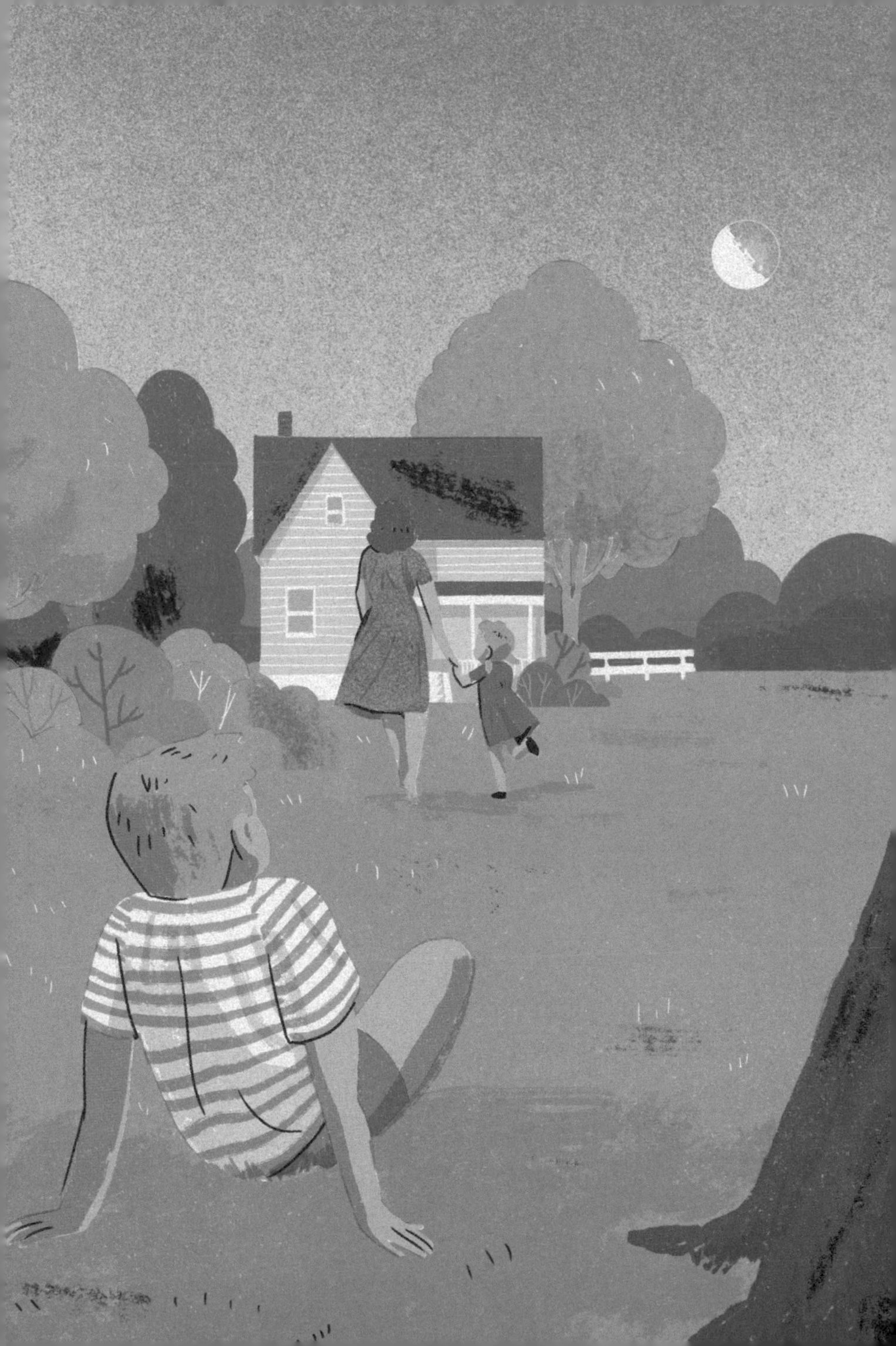

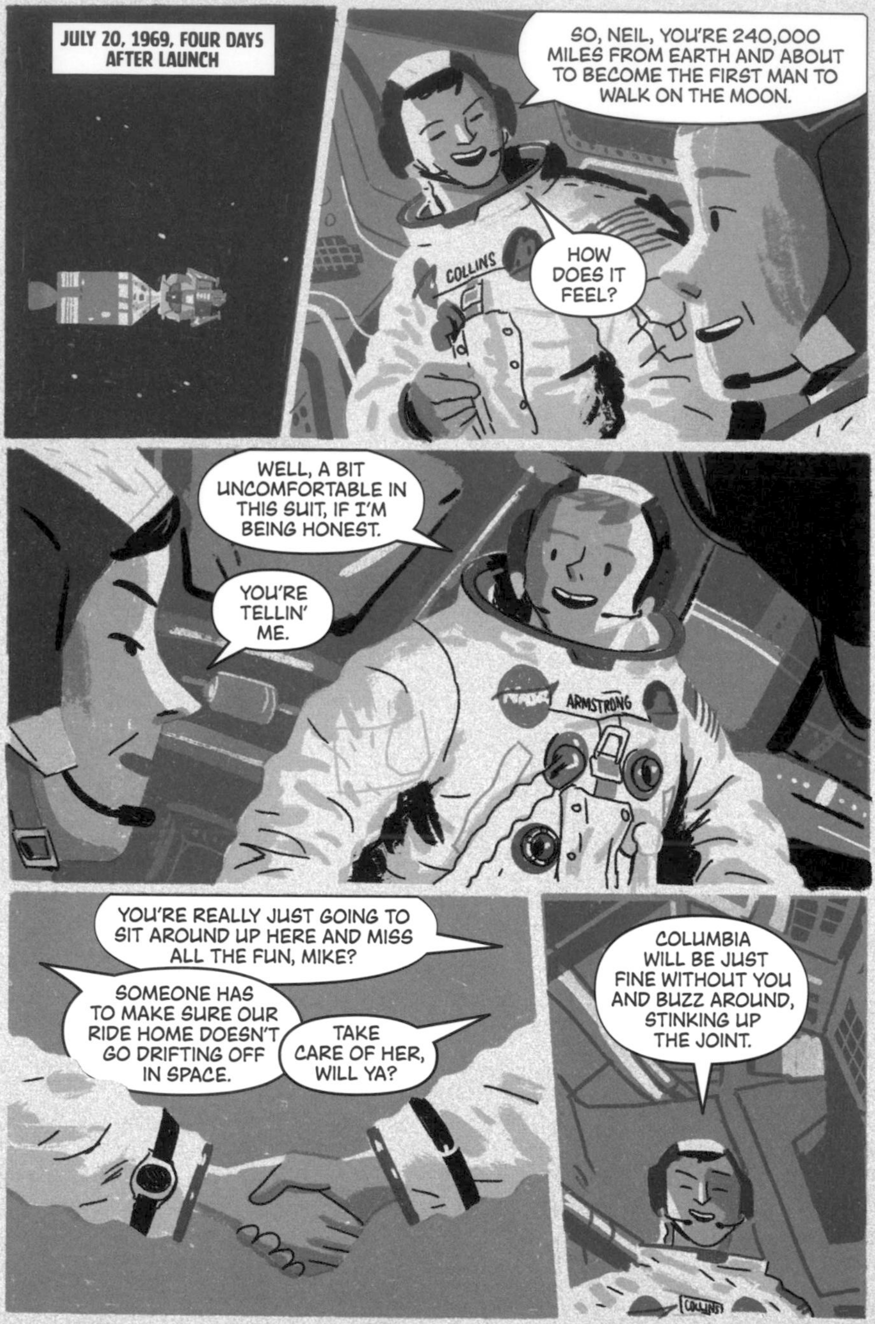
JULY 20, 1969, FOUR DAYS AFTER LAUNCH
SO, NEIL, YOU'RE 240,000 MILES FROM EARTH AND ABOUT TO BECOME THE FIRST MAN TO WALK ON THE MOON.
HOW DOES IT FEEL?
COLLINS
WELL, A BIT UNCOMFORTABLE IN THIS SUIT, IF I'M BEING HONEST.
YOU'RE TELLIN' ME.
ARMSTRONG
YOU'RE REALLY JUST GOING TO SIT AROUND UP HERE AND MISS ALL THE FUN, MIKE?
SOMEONE HAS TO MAKE SURE OUR RIDE HOME DOESN'T GO DRIFTING OFF IN SPACE.
TAKE CARE OF HER, WILL YA?
COLUMBIA WILL BE JUST FINE WITHOUT YOU AND BUZZ AROUND, STINKING UP THE JOINT.
COLLINS

WELCOME TO THE EAGLE LANDER. DESTINATION: THE MOON.

READY?

READY.

ALDRIN

GOT SOME WORK AHEAD OF US BEFORE WE CAN GO ANYWHERE.

LOOKS LIKE YOU HAVE THE COMPUTER CHECKS COVERED, SO I'LL INSPECT THE ASCENT ENGINE.

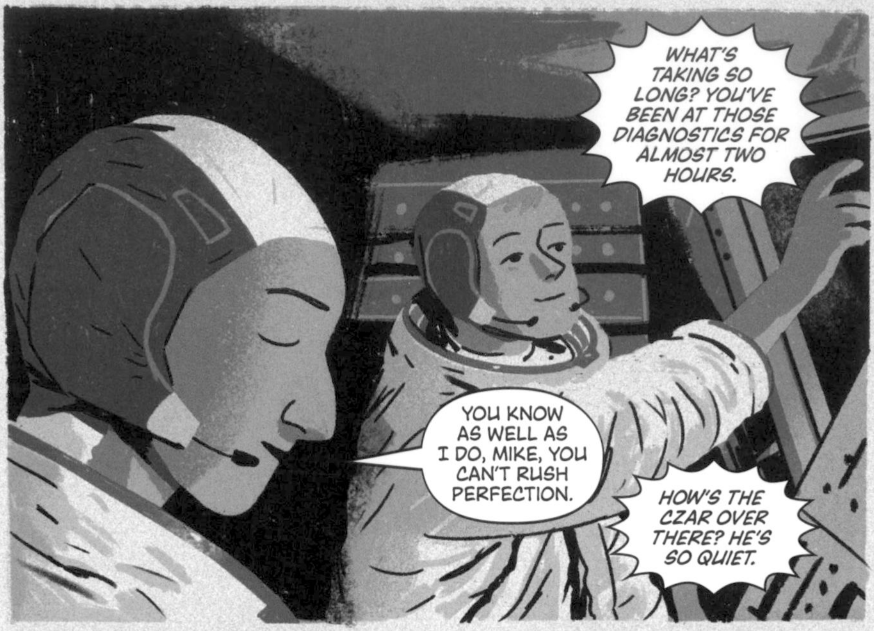
WHAT'S TAKING SO LONG? YOU'VE BEEN AT THOSE DIAGNOSTICS FOR ALMOST TWO HOURS.
YOU KNOW AS WELL AS I DO, MIKE, YOU CAN'T RUSH PERFECTION.
HOW'S THE CZAR OVER THERE? HE'S SO QUIET.

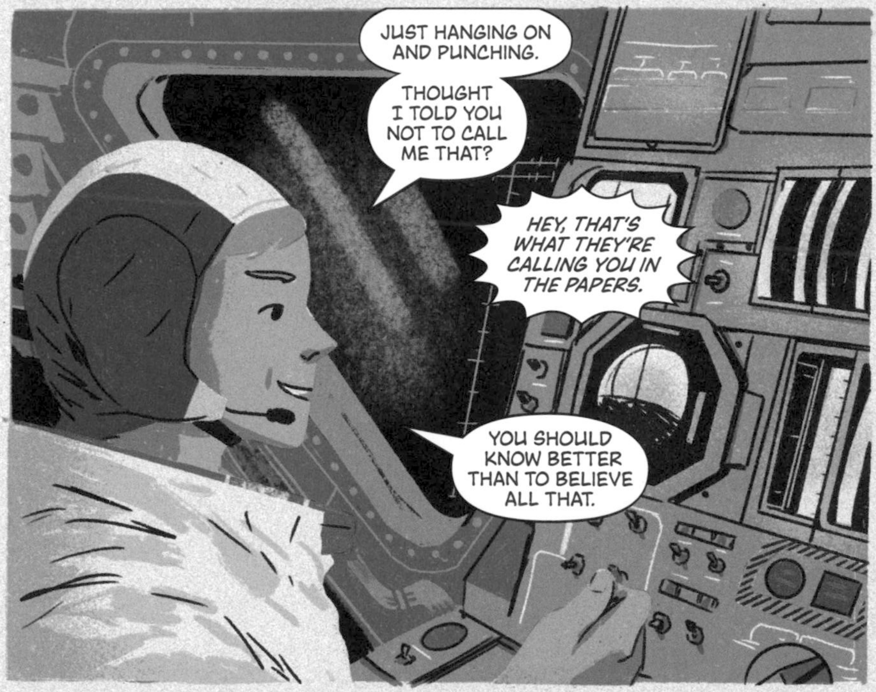
JUST HANGING ON AND PUNCHING.
THOUGHT I TOLD YOU NOT TO CALL ME THAT?
HEY, THAT'S WHAT THEY'RE CALLING YOU IN THE PAPERS.
YOU SHOULD KNOW BETTER THAN TO BELIEVE ALL THAT.

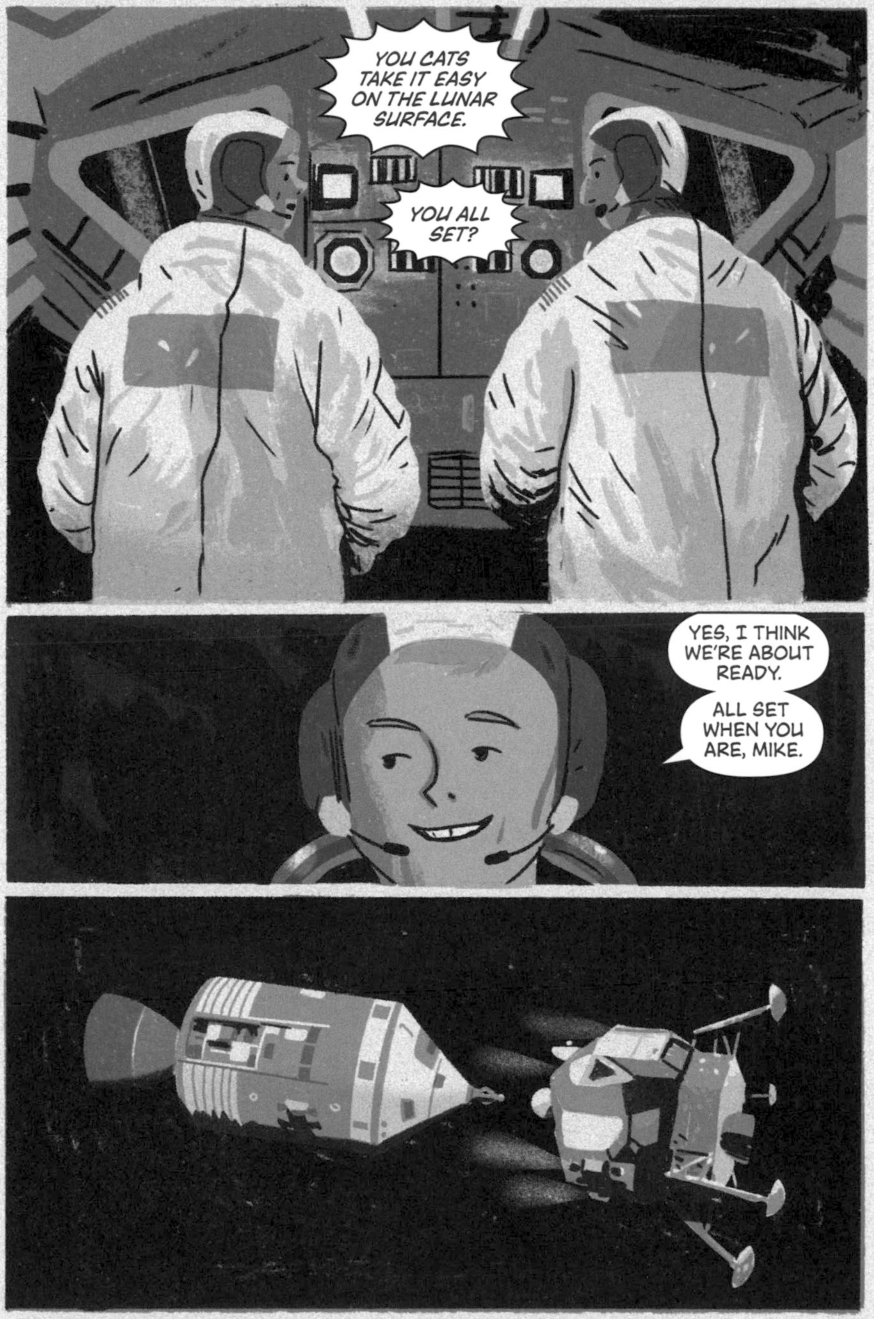
YOU CATS TAKE IT EASY ON THE LUNAR SURFACE.
YOU ALL SET?
YES, I THINK WE'RE ABOUT READY.
ALL SET WHEN YOU ARE, MIKE.

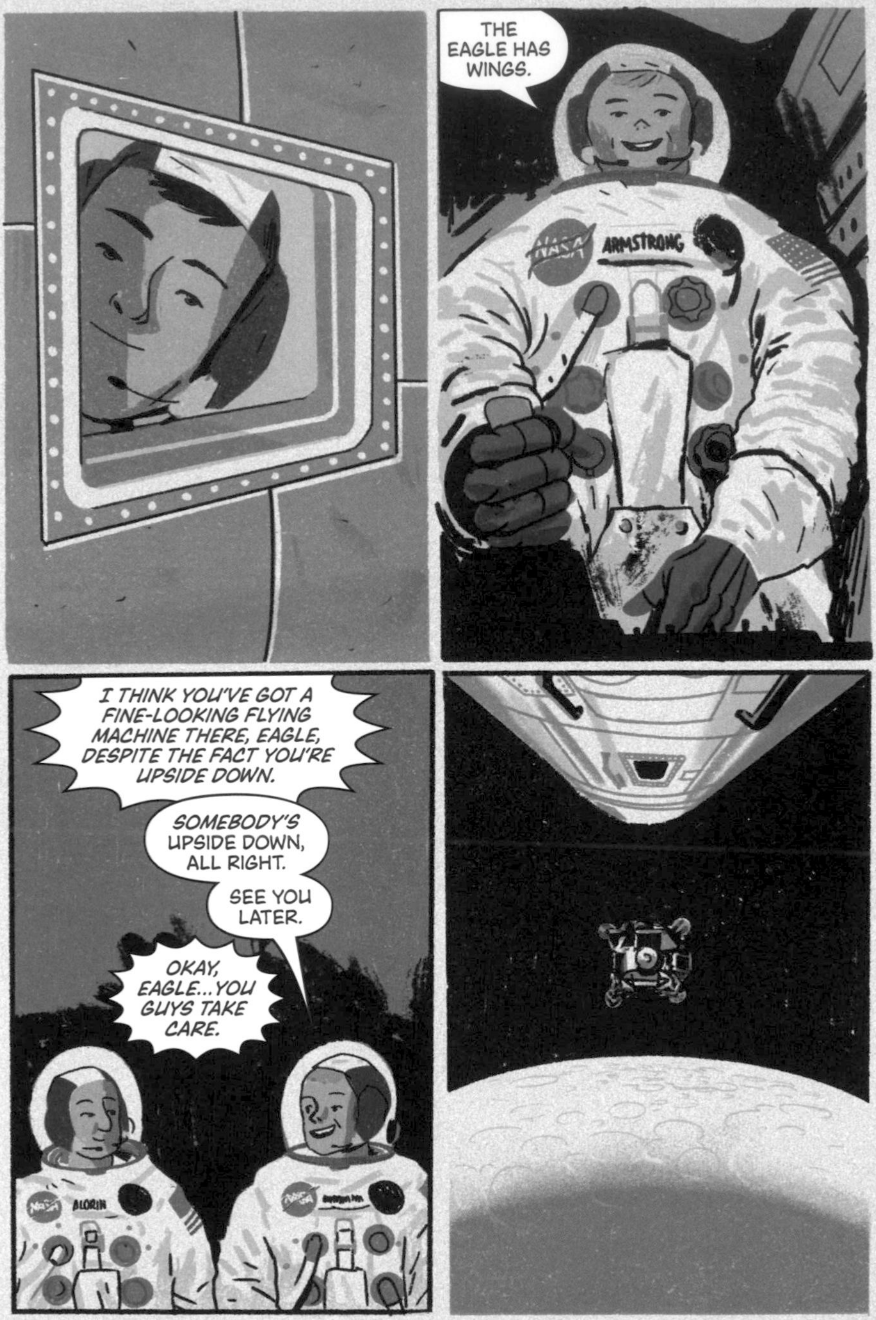
THE EAGLE HAS WINGS.
NASA
ARMSTRONG
I THINK YOU'VE GOT A FINE-LOOKING FLYING MACHINE THERE, EAGLE, DESPITE THE FACT YOU'RE UPSIDE DOWN.
SOMEBODY'S UPSIDE DOWN, ALL RIGHT.
SEE YOU LATER.
OKAY, EAGLE...YOU GUYS TAKE CARE.

Michael Collins

Michael Collins was born on October 31, 1930, in Rome, Italy, where his father, Major General James Collins, was stationed in the military. Curious and very clever, Michael loved to read and enjoyed building model planes. He played on his high-school football team and went on to attend the United States Military Academy at West Point, where he graduated with a bachelor of science in 1952.

Michael served as a fighter pilot as well as an experimental test pilot prior to being selected to join the third group of NASA astronauts in 1963. With NASA, he was the pilot of Gemini 10, a mission in which he became just the third American ever to complete an EVA (extravehicular activity). Or, to put it in simpler and cooler terms, he spacewalked!

For the Apollo 11 mission, Michael became the pilot of Columbia, the command module that stayed behind while Neil and Buzz completed their journey to the moon. After the mission, Michael received the 1969 Presidential Medal of Freedom and was also awarded the 2011 Congressional Gold Medal, two of the highest awards a civilian can receive in the United States.

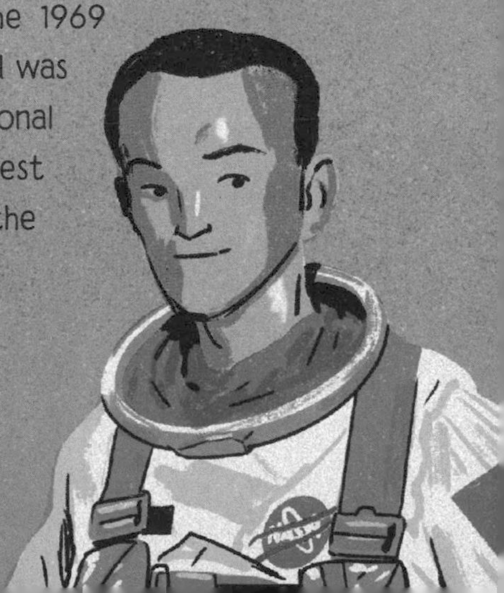

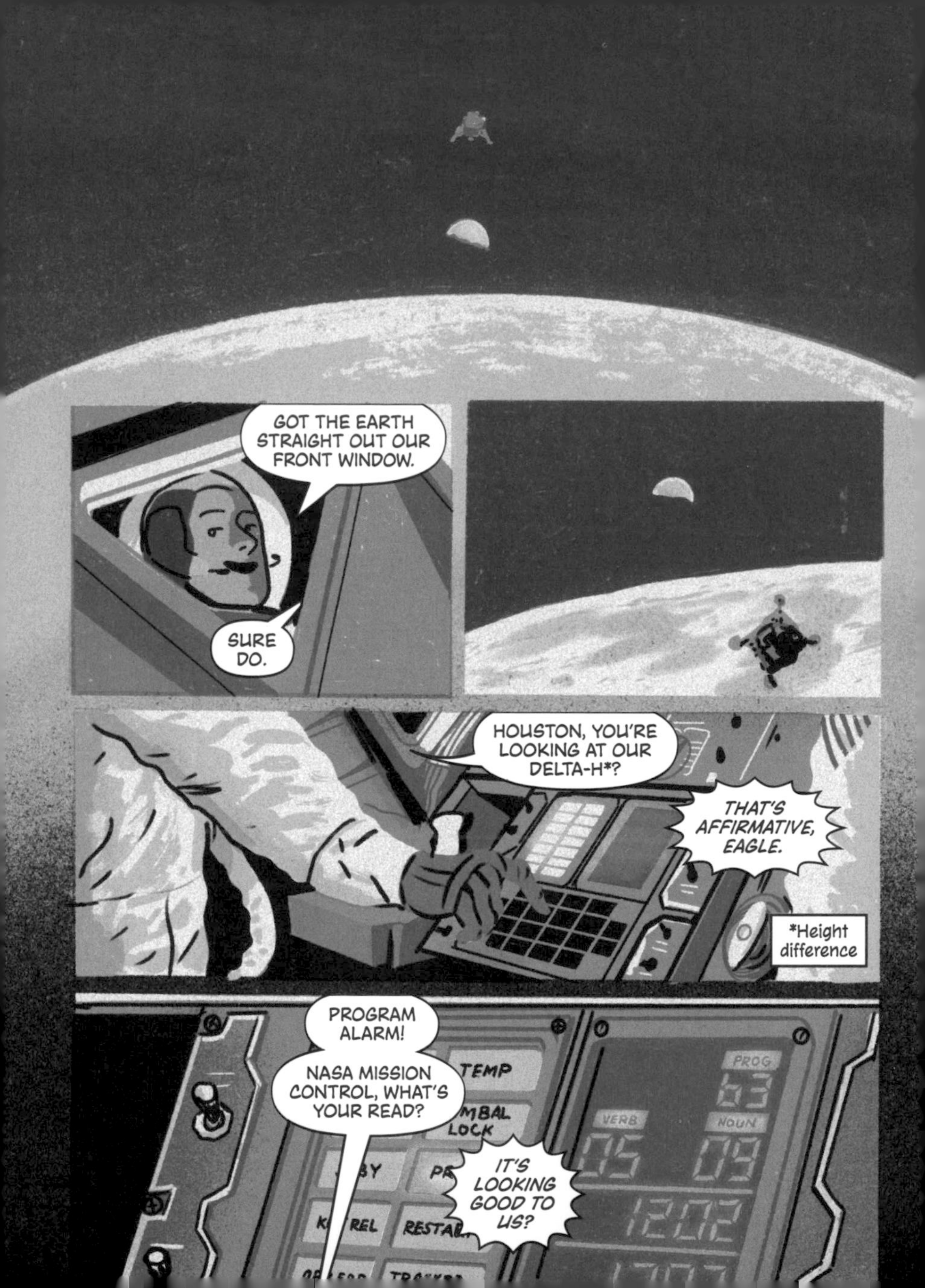
GOT THE EARTH STRAIGHT OUT OUR FRONT WINDOW.
SURE DO.
HOUSTON, YOU'RE LOOKING AT OUR DELTA-H*?
THAT'S AFFIRMATIVE, EAGLE.
*Height difference
PROGRAM ALARM!
NASA MISSION CONTROL, WHAT'S YOUR READ?
IT'S LOOKING GOOD TO US?
TEMP
LOCK
PROG
63
VERB
NOUN
05
09
1202

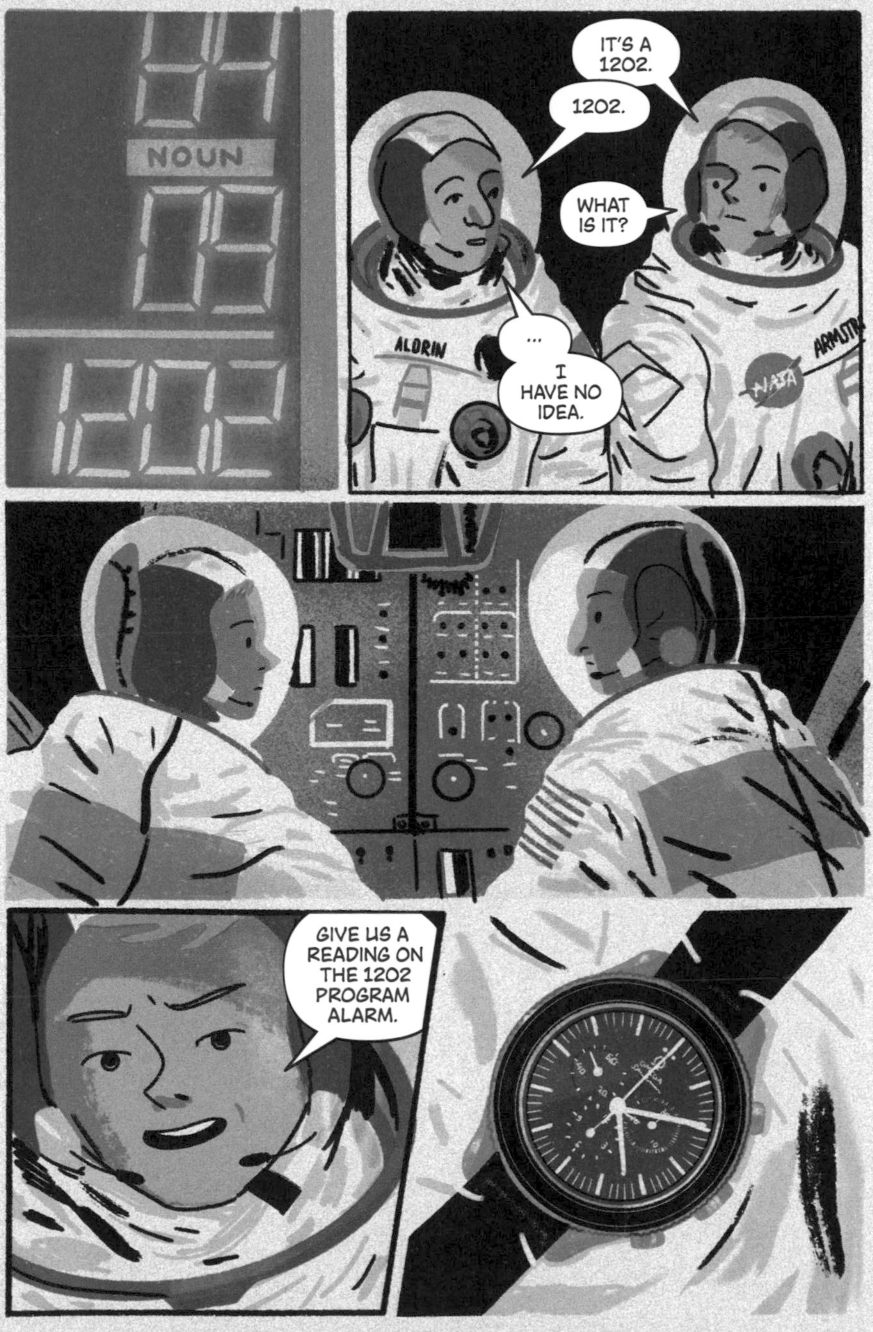
NOUN
IT'S A 1202.
1202.
WHAT IS IT?
...
I HAVE NO IDEA.
ALDRIN
GIVE US A READING ON THE 1202 PROGRAM ALARM.

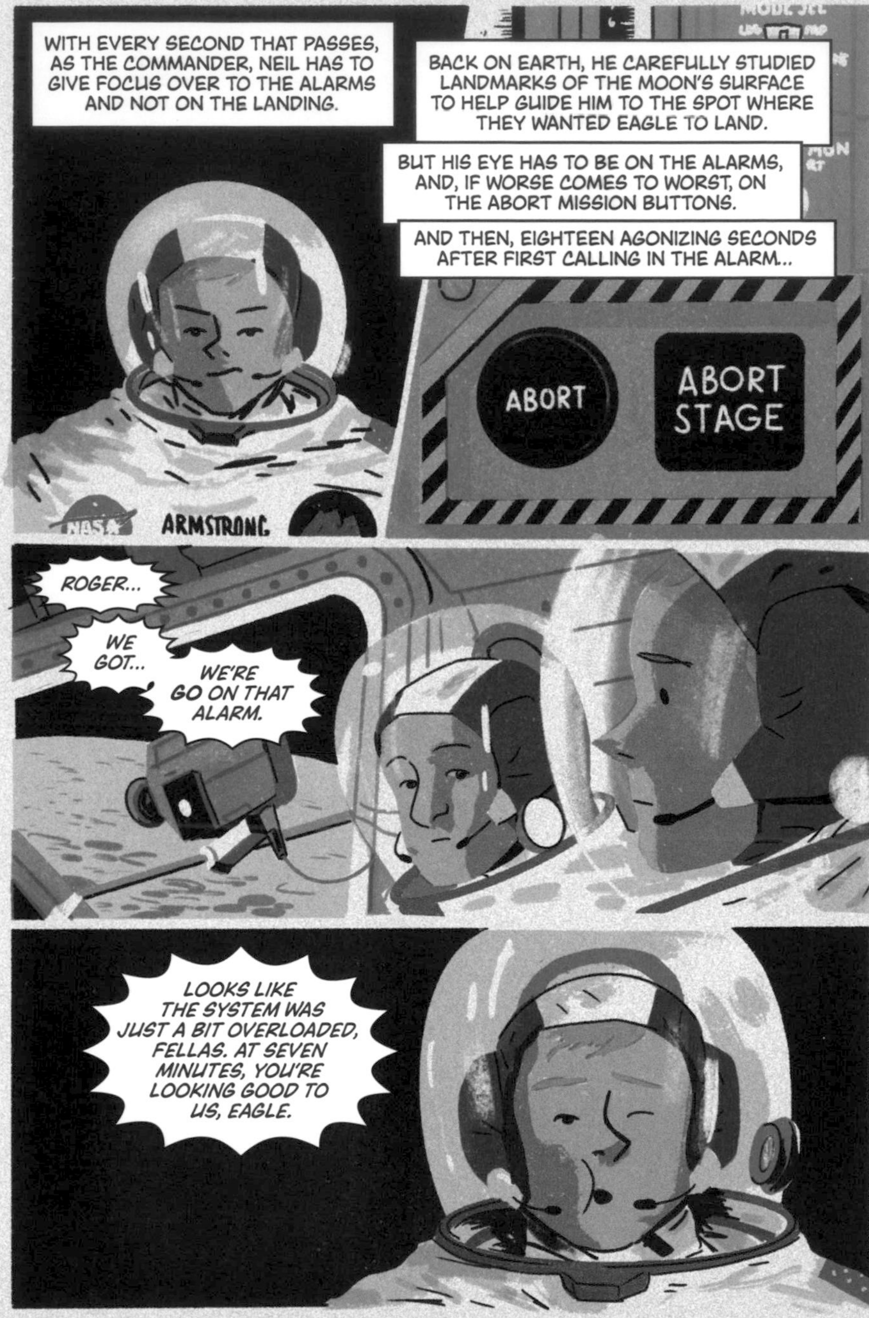

WITH EVERY SECOND THAT PASSES, AS THE COMMANDER, NEIL HAS TO GIVE FOCUS OVER TO THE ALARMS AND NOT ON THE LANDING.
BACK ON EARTH, HE CAREFULLY STUDIED LANDMARKS OF THE MOON'S SURFACE TO HELP GUIDE HIM TO THE SPOT WHERE THEY WANTED EAGLE TO LAND.
BUT HIS EYE HAS TO BE ON THE ALARMS, AND, IF WORSE COMES TO WORST, ON THE ABORT MISSION BUTTONS.
AND THEN, EIGHTEEN AGONIZING SECONDS AFTER FIRST CALLING IN THE ALARM...
ABORT
ABORT STAGE
NASA
ARMSTRONG
ROGER...
WE GOT...
WE'RE GO ON THAT ALARM.
LOOKS LIKE THE SYSTEM WAS JUST A BIT OVERLOADED, FELLAS. AT SEVEN MINUTES, YOU'RE LOOKING GOOD TO US, EAGLE.

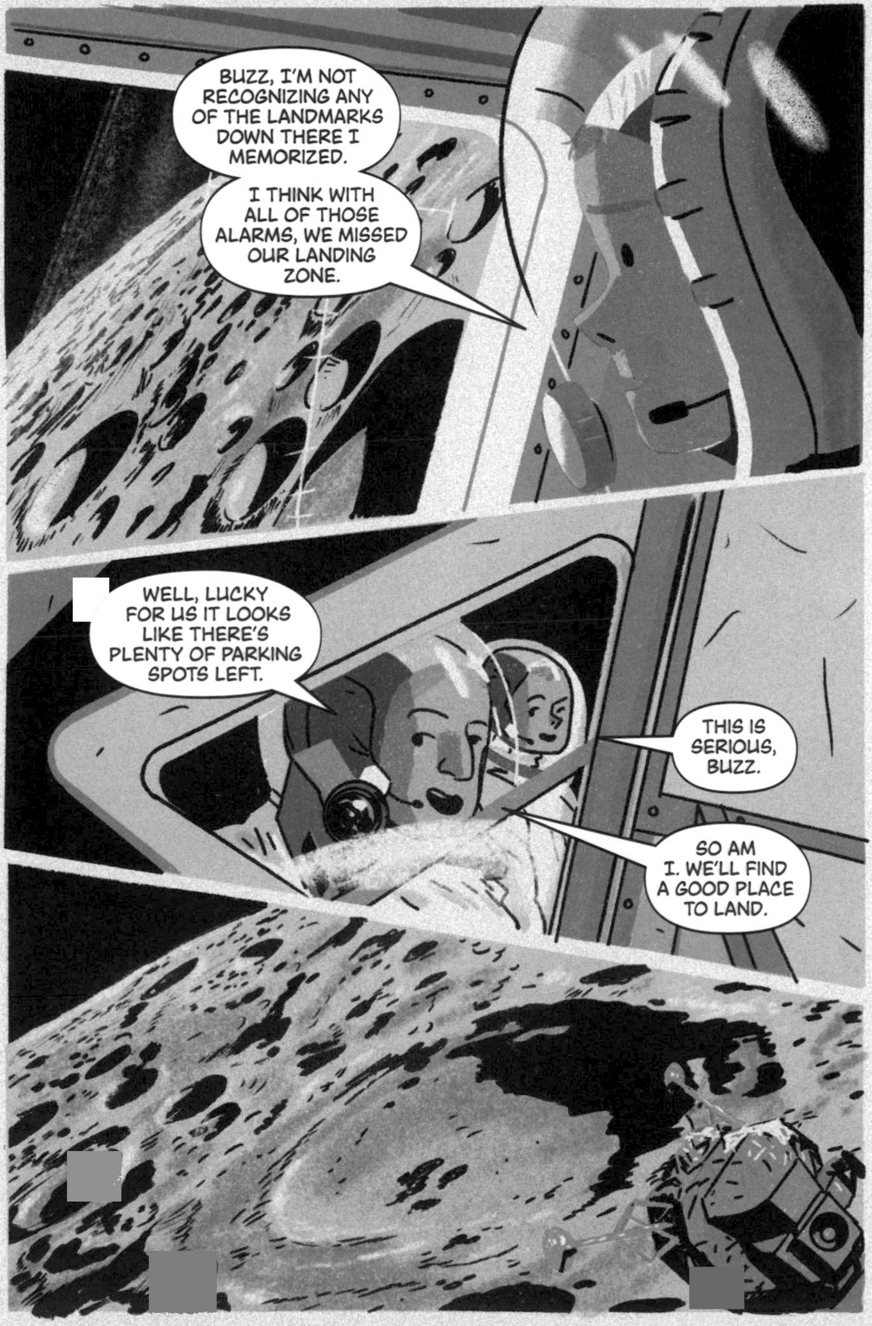
BUZZ, I'M NOT RECOGNIZING ANY OF THE LANDMARKS DOWN THERE I MEMORIZED.
I THINK WITH ALL OF THOSE ALARMS, WE MISSED OUR LANDING ZONE.
WELL, LUCKY FOR US IT LOOKS LIKE THERE'S PLENTY OF PARKING SPOTS LEFT.
THIS IS SERIOUS, BUZZ.
SO AM I. WE'LL FIND A GOOD PLACE TO LAND.

Eagle, the Apollo 11 Lunar Module

Designed for the sole purpose of landing on and taking off from the moon, the lunar module (known as Eagle for the Apollo 11 mission) was actually two different spacecrafts put together: one to land on the moon and the other to rejoin Columbia and go back home.

Inside, there were no seats for the astronauts because the craft had to be light enough to fly. In fact, Neil and Buzz were standing for the whole flight. Another way NASA engineers reduced weight was by cutting down the size of the windows. So by the time that Neil and Buzz were standing at the controls, there was not much space for the astronauts to even look outside.

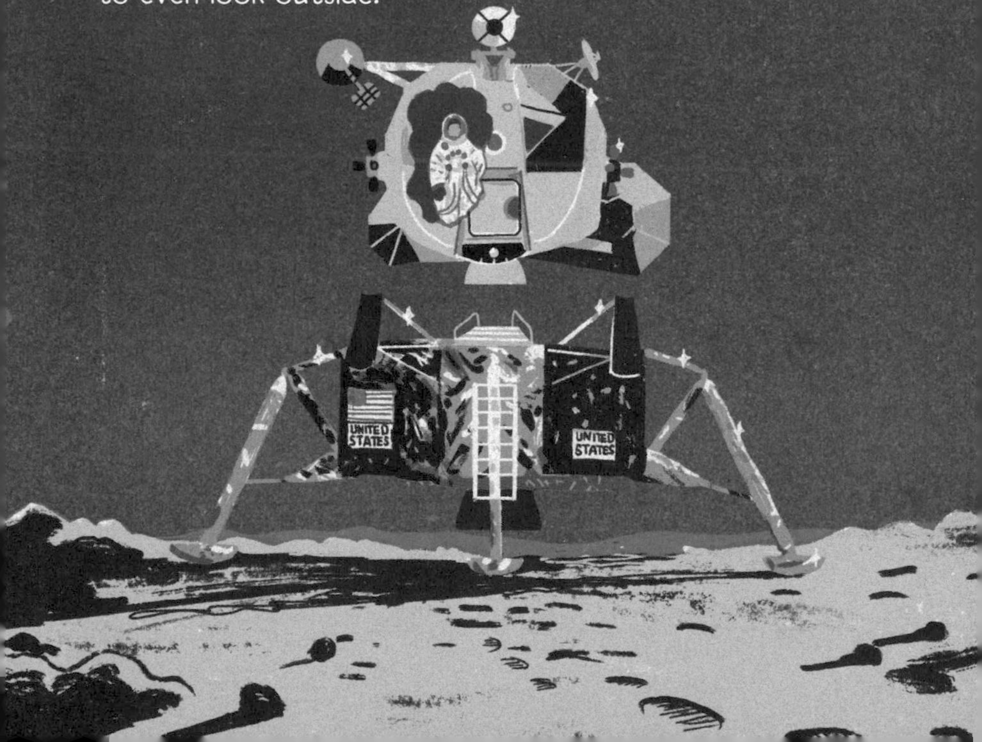
UNITED STATES
UNITED STATES

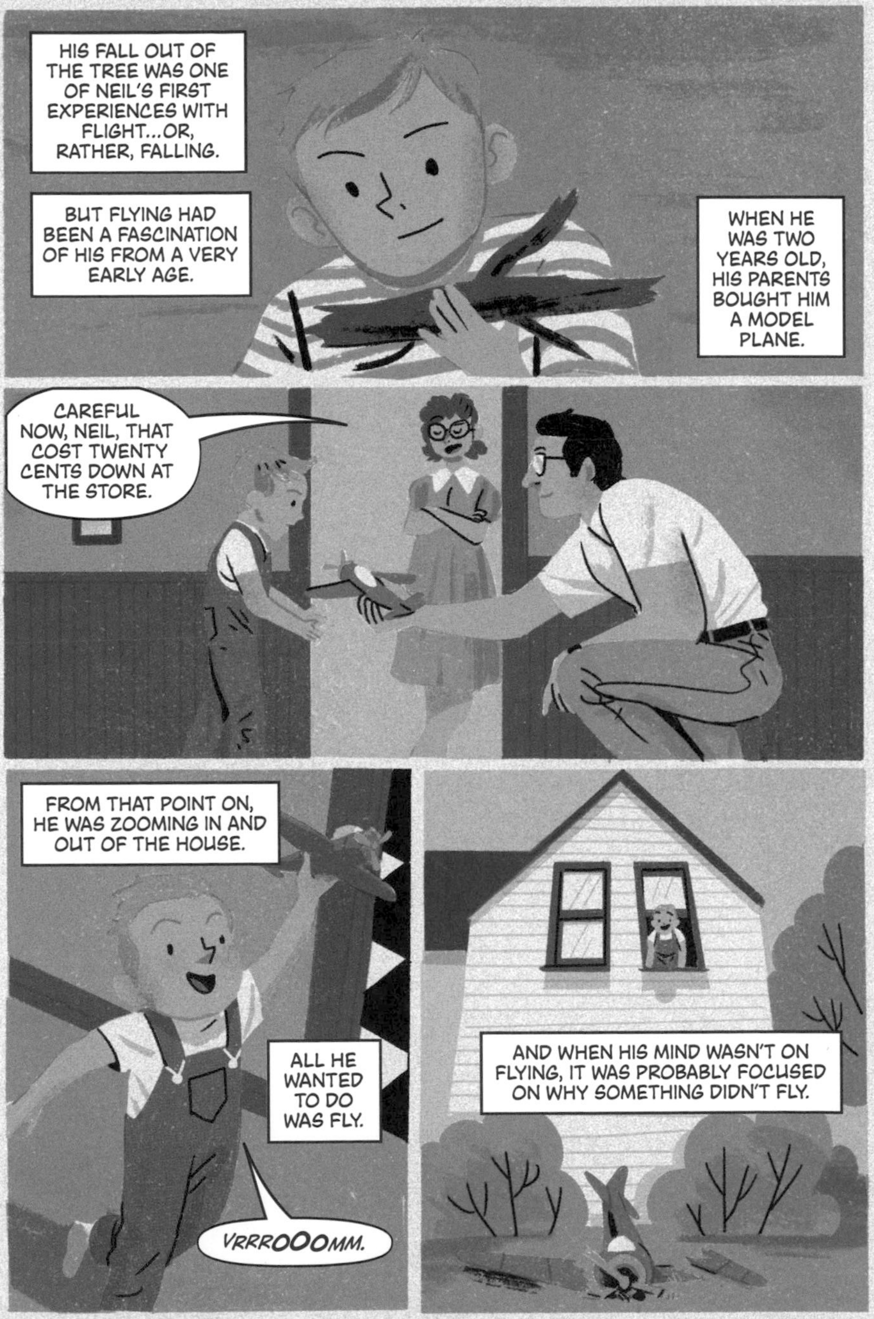
HIS FALL OUT OF THE TREE WAS ONE OF NEIL'S FIRST EXPERIENCES WITH FLIGHT...OR, RATHER, FALLING.
BUT FLYING HAD BEEN A FASCINATION OF HIS FROM A VERY EARLY AGE.
WHEN HE WAS TWO YEARS OLD, HIS PARENTS BOUGHT HIM A MODEL PLANE.
CAREFUL NOW, NEIL, THAT COST TWENTY CENTS DOWN AT THE STORE.
FROM THAT POINT ON, HE WAS ZOOMING IN AND OUT OF THE HOUSE.
ALL HE WANTED TO DO WAS FLY.
VRRROOOMM.
AND WHEN HIS MIND WASN'T ON FLYING, IT WAS PROBABLY FOCUSED ON WHY SOMETHING DIDN'T FLY.

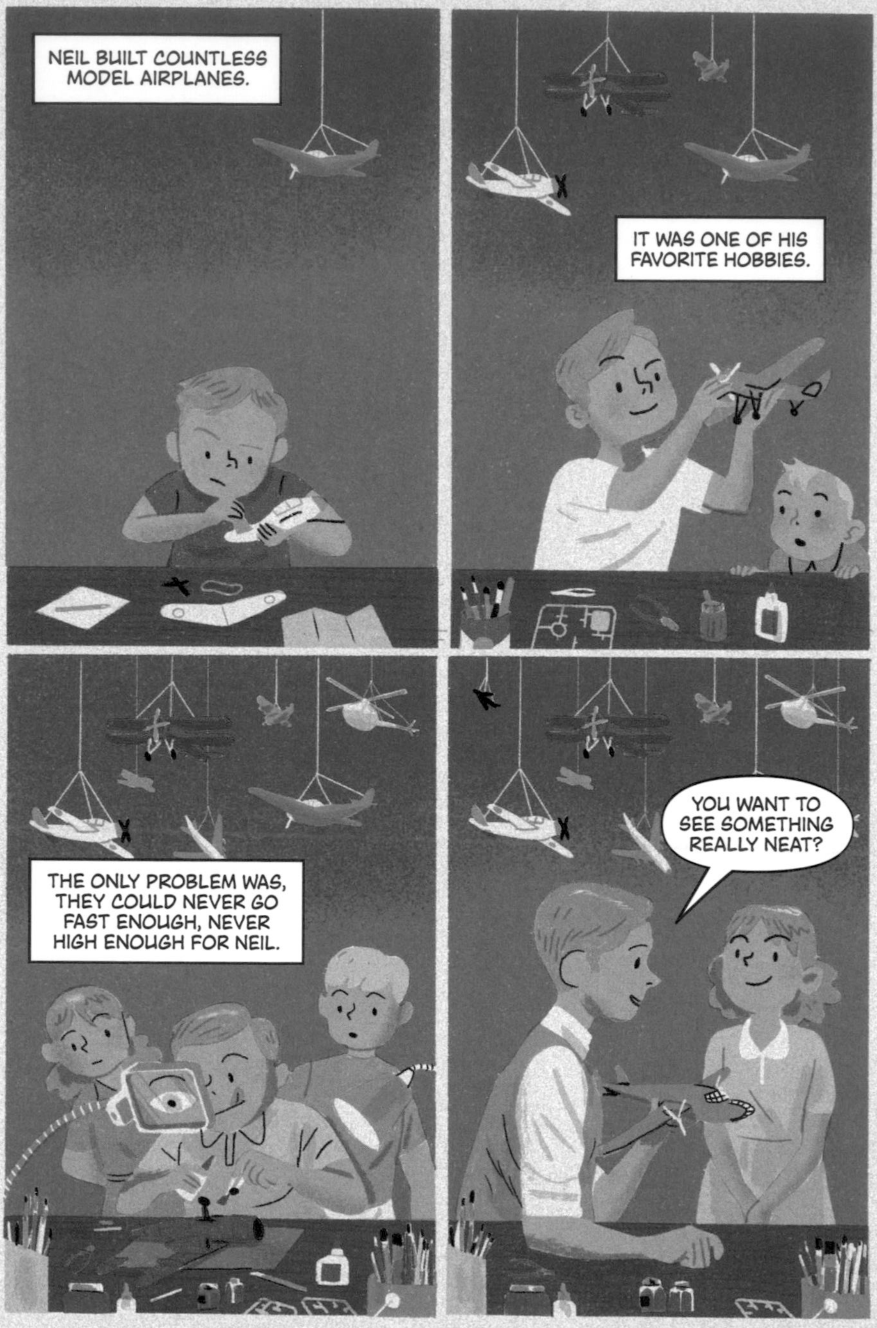
NEIL BUILT COUNTLESS MODEL AIRPLANES.
IT WAS ONE OF HIS FAVORITE HOBBIES.
THE ONLY PROBLEM WAS, THEY COULD NEVER GO FAST ENOUGH, NEVER HIGH ENOUGH FOR NEIL.
YOU WANT TO SEE SOMETHING REALLY NEAT?

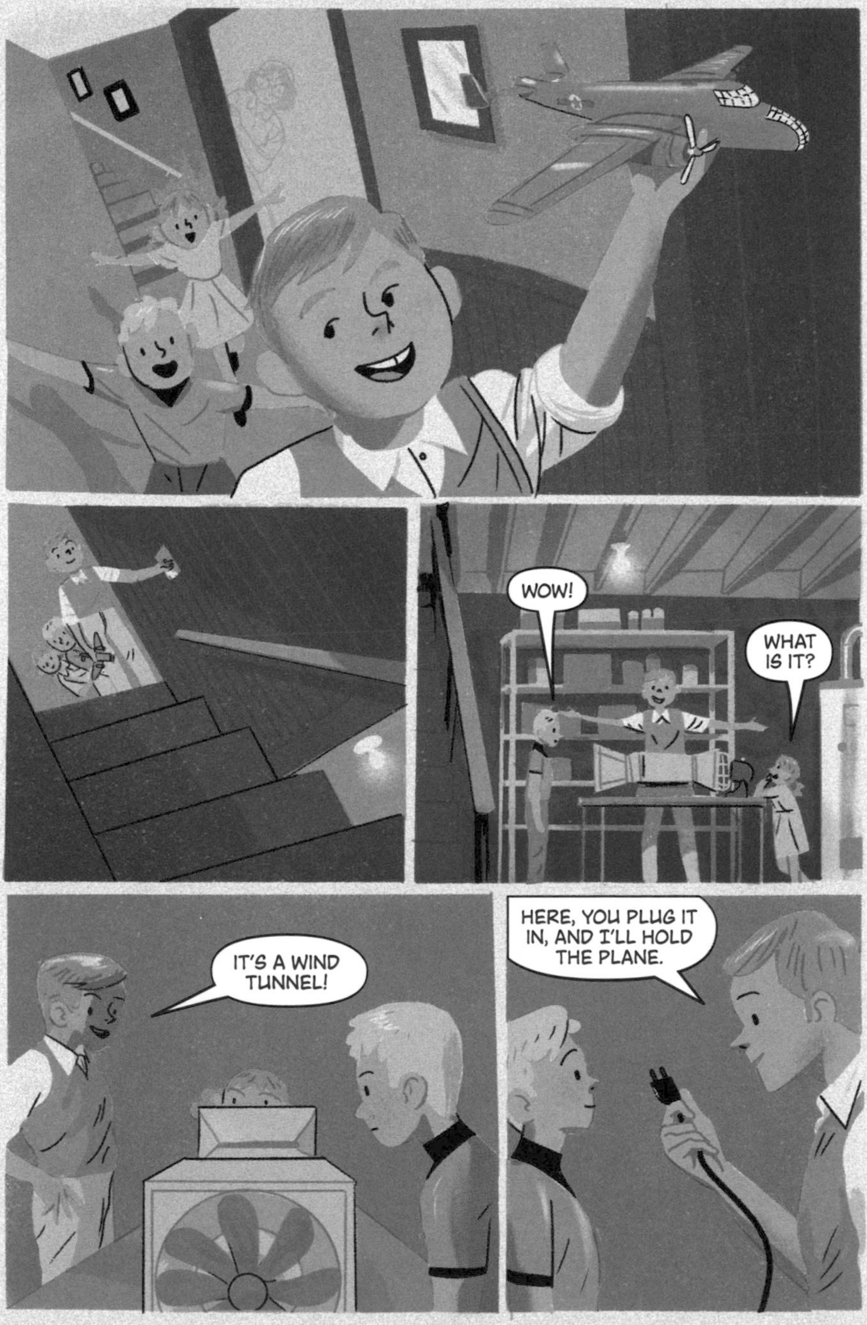
WOW!
WHAT IS IT?
IT'S A WIND TUNNEL!
HERE, YOU PLUG IT IN, AND I'LL HOLD THE PLANE.

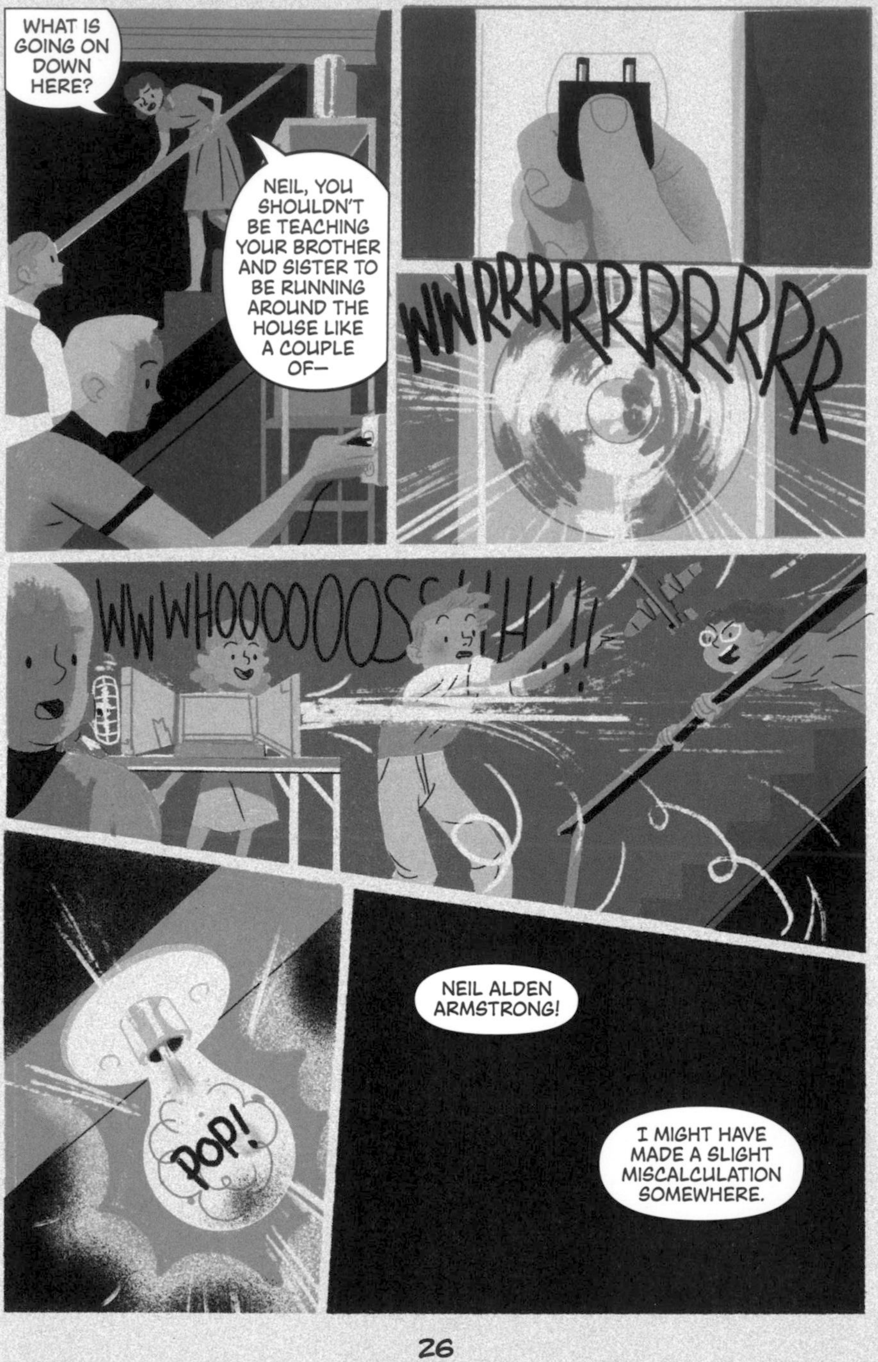
WHAT IS GOING ON DOWN HERE?
NEIL, YOU SHOULDN'T BE TEACHING YOUR BROTHER AND SISTER TO BE RUNNING AROUND THE HOUSE LIKE A COUPLE OF—
WWRRRRRRRRRRRR
WWWHOOOOOOSSHH!!
POP!
NEIL ALDEN ARMSTRONG!
I MIGHT HAVE MADE A SLIGHT MISCALCULATION SOMEWHERE.

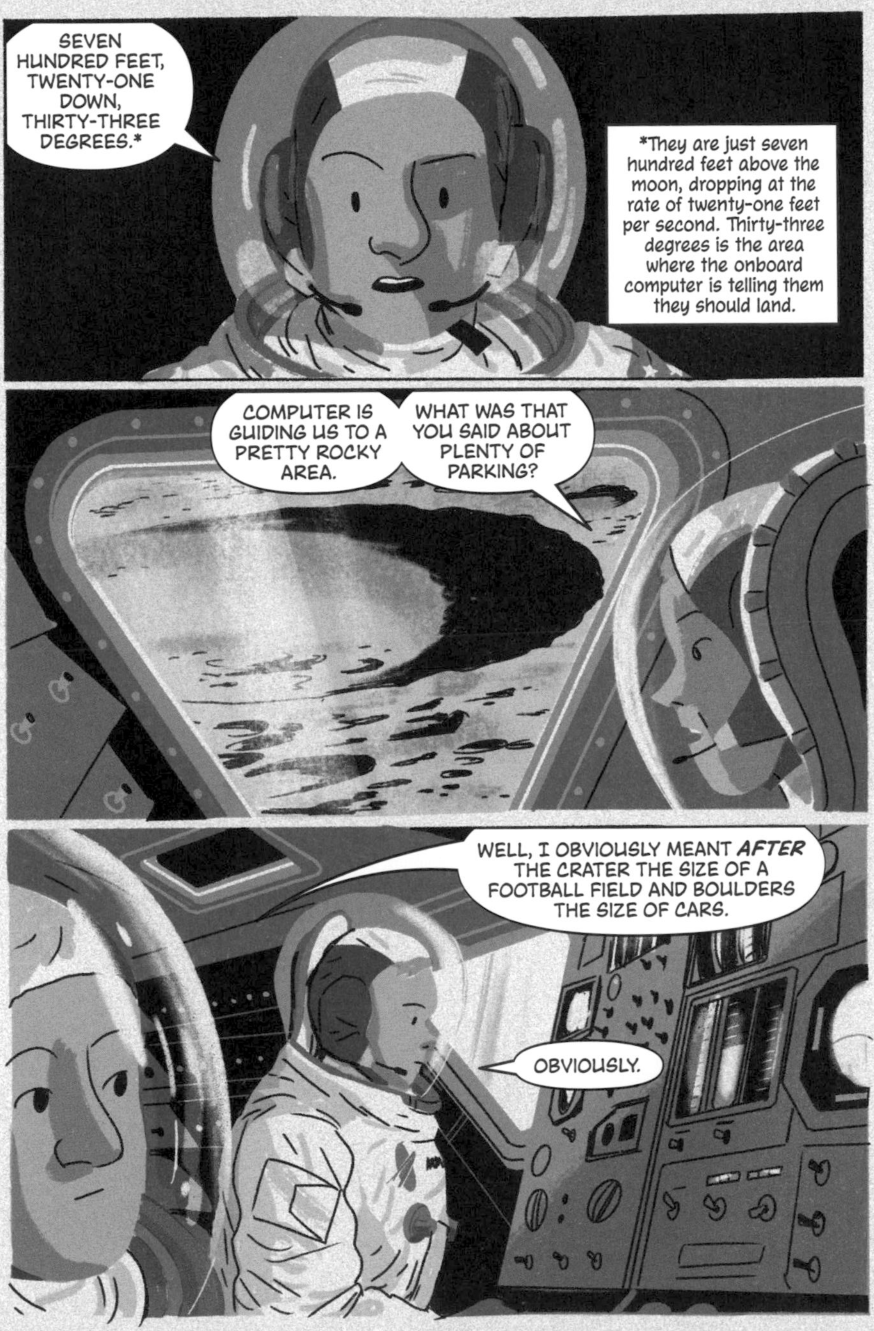
SEVEN HUNDRED FEET, TWENTY-ONE DOWN, THIRTY-THREE DEGREES.*
*They are just seven hundred feet above the moon, dropping at the rate of twenty-one feet per second. Thirty-three degrees is the area where the onboard computer is telling them they should land.
COMPUTER IS GUIDING US TO A PRETTY ROCKY AREA.
WHAT WAS THAT YOU SAID ABOUT PLENTY OF PARKING?
WELL, I OBVIOUSLY MEANT *AFTER* THE CRATER THE SIZE OF A FOOTBALL FIELD AND BOULDERS THE SIZE OF CARS.
OBVIOUSLY.

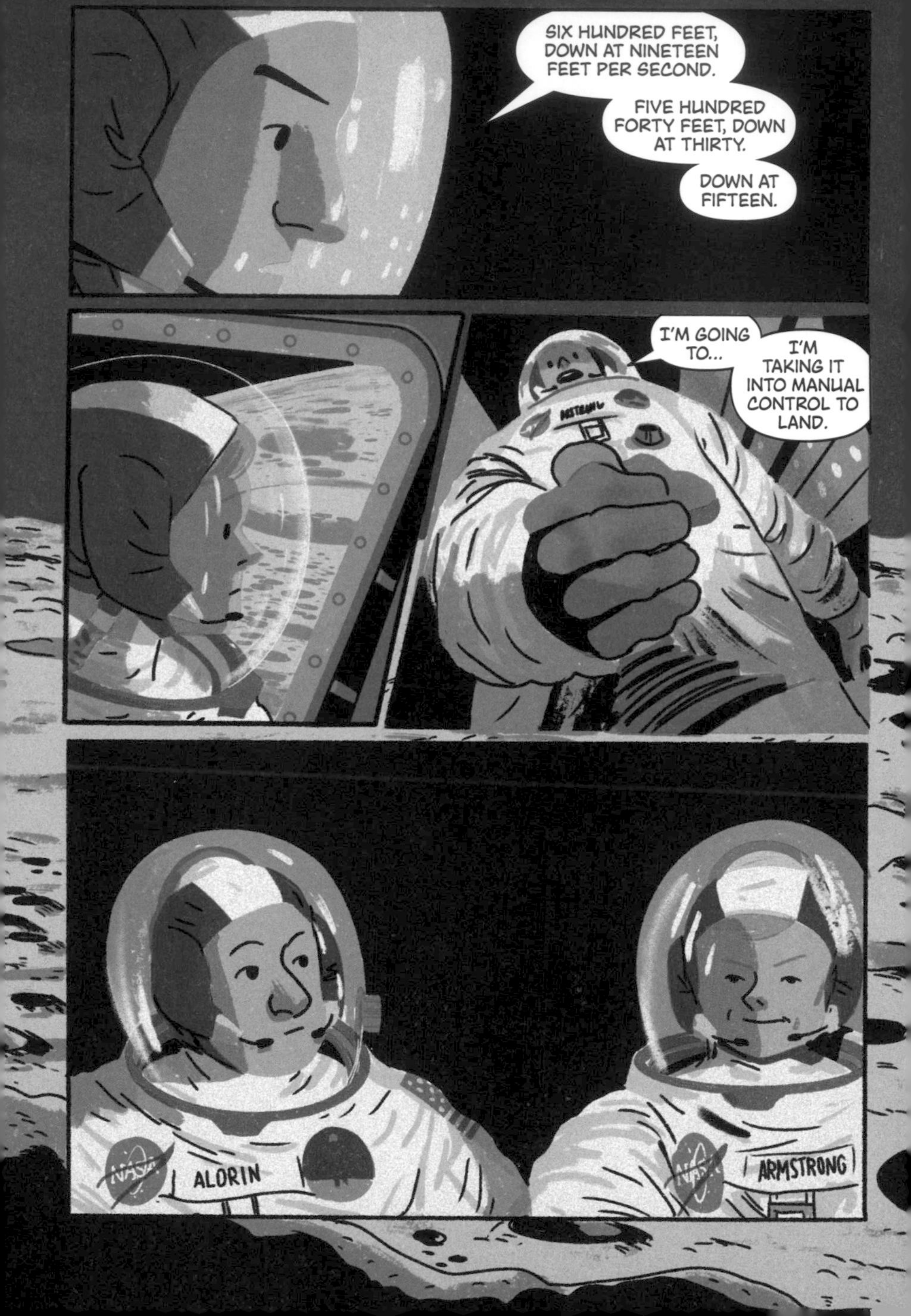

SIX HUNDRED FEET, DOWN AT NINETEEN FEET PER SECOND.
FIVE HUNDRED FORTY FEET, DOWN AT THIRTY.
DOWN AT FIFTEEN.
I'M GOING TO...
I'M TAKING IT INTO MANUAL CONTROL TO LAND.
ALDRIN
ARMSTRONG

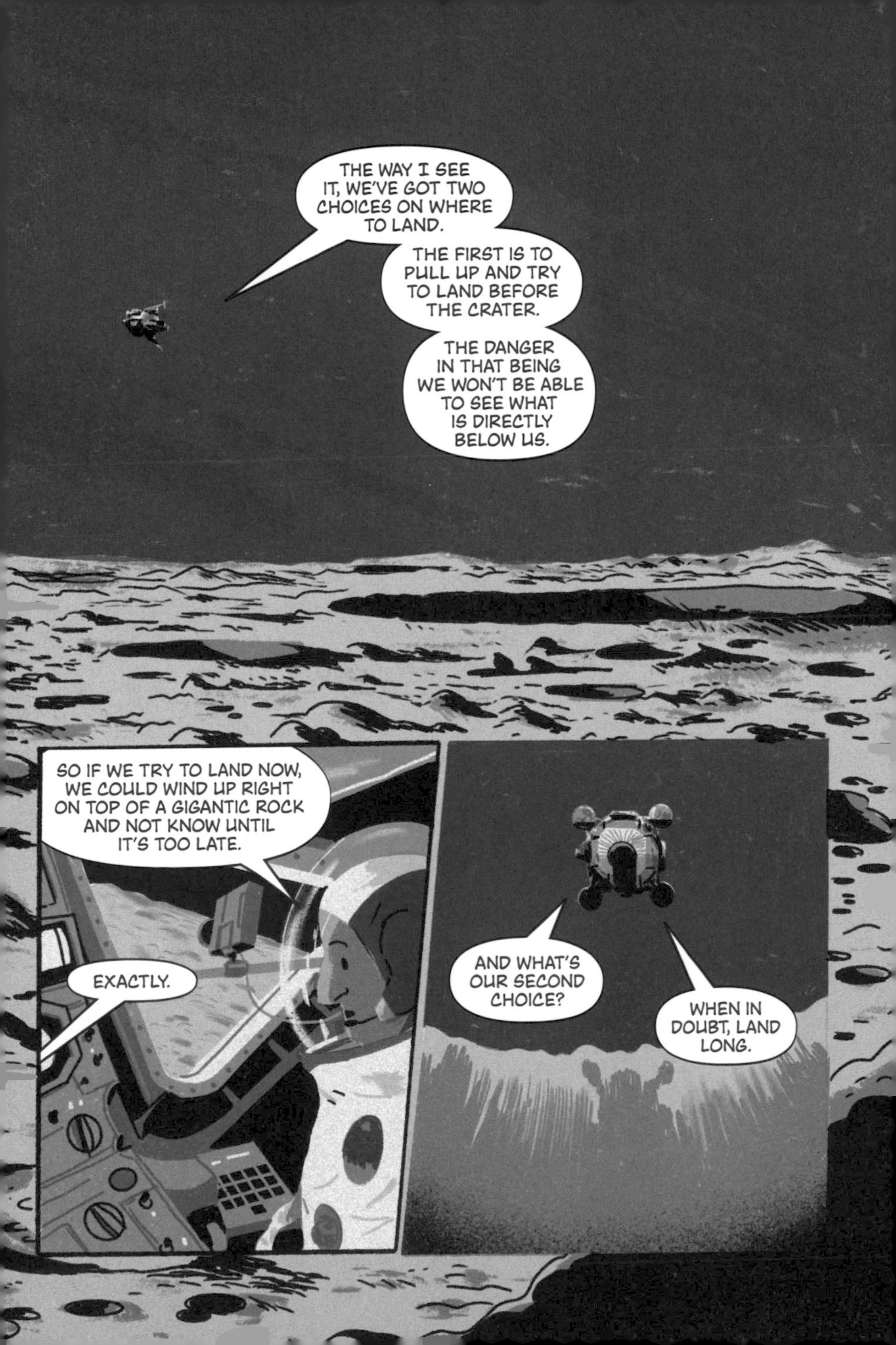

THE WAY I SEE IT, WE'VE GOT TWO CHOICES ON WHERE TO LAND.
THE FIRST IS TO PULL UP AND TRY TO LAND BEFORE THE CRATER.
THE DANGER IN THAT BEING WE WON'T BE ABLE TO SEE WHAT IS DIRECTLY BELOW US.
SO IF WE TRY TO LAND NOW, WE COULD WIND UP RIGHT ON TOP OF A GIGANTIC ROCK AND NOT KNOW UNTIL IT'S TOO LATE.
EXACTLY.
AND WHAT'S OUR SECOND CHOICE?
WHEN IN DOUBT, LAND LONG.

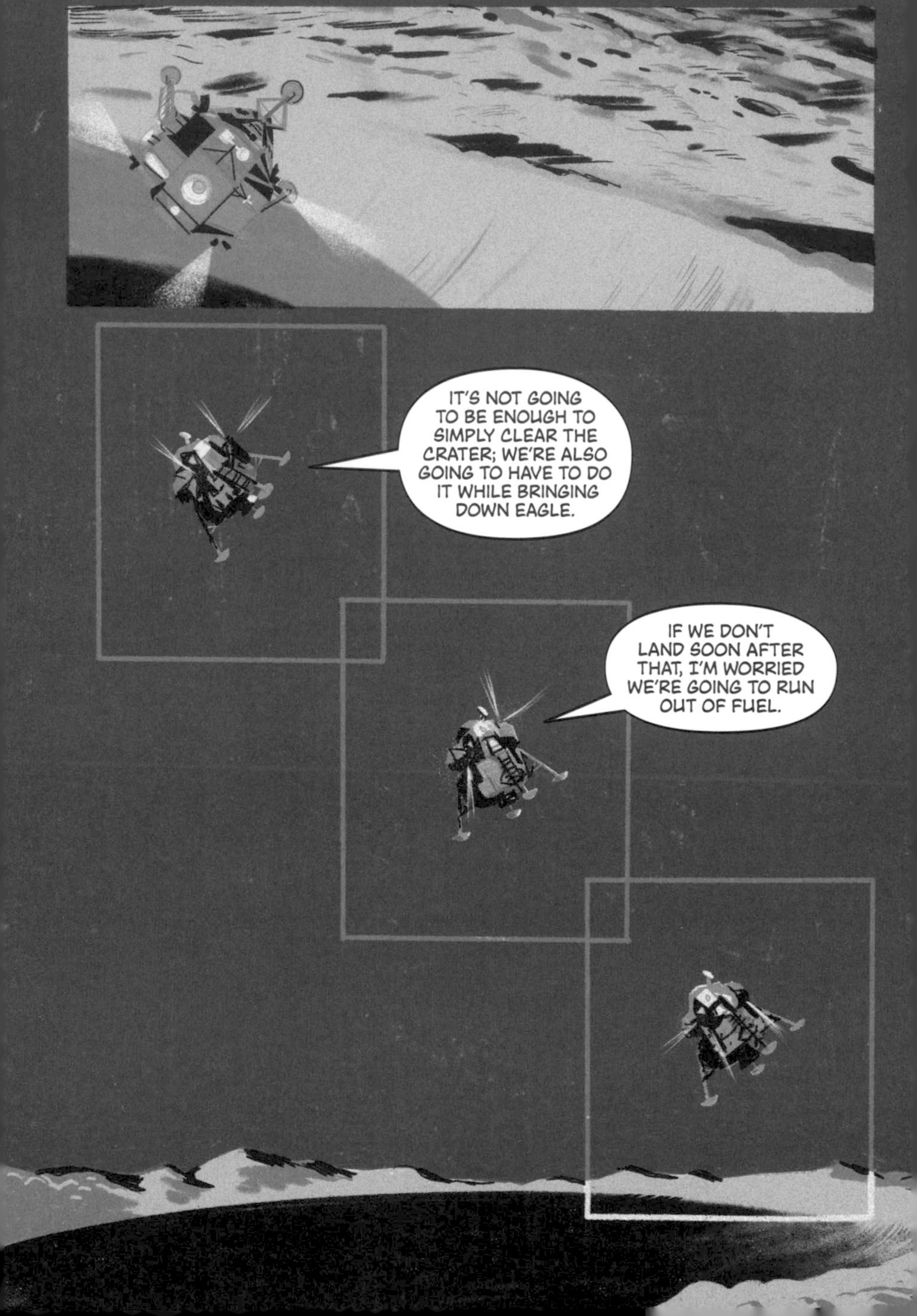
IT'S NOT GOING TO BE ENOUGH TO SIMPLY CLEAR THE CRATER; WE'RE ALSO GOING TO HAVE TO DO IT WHILE BRINGING DOWN EAGLE.
IF WE DON'T LAND SOON AFTER THAT, I'M WORRIED WE'RE GOING TO RUN OUT OF FUEL.

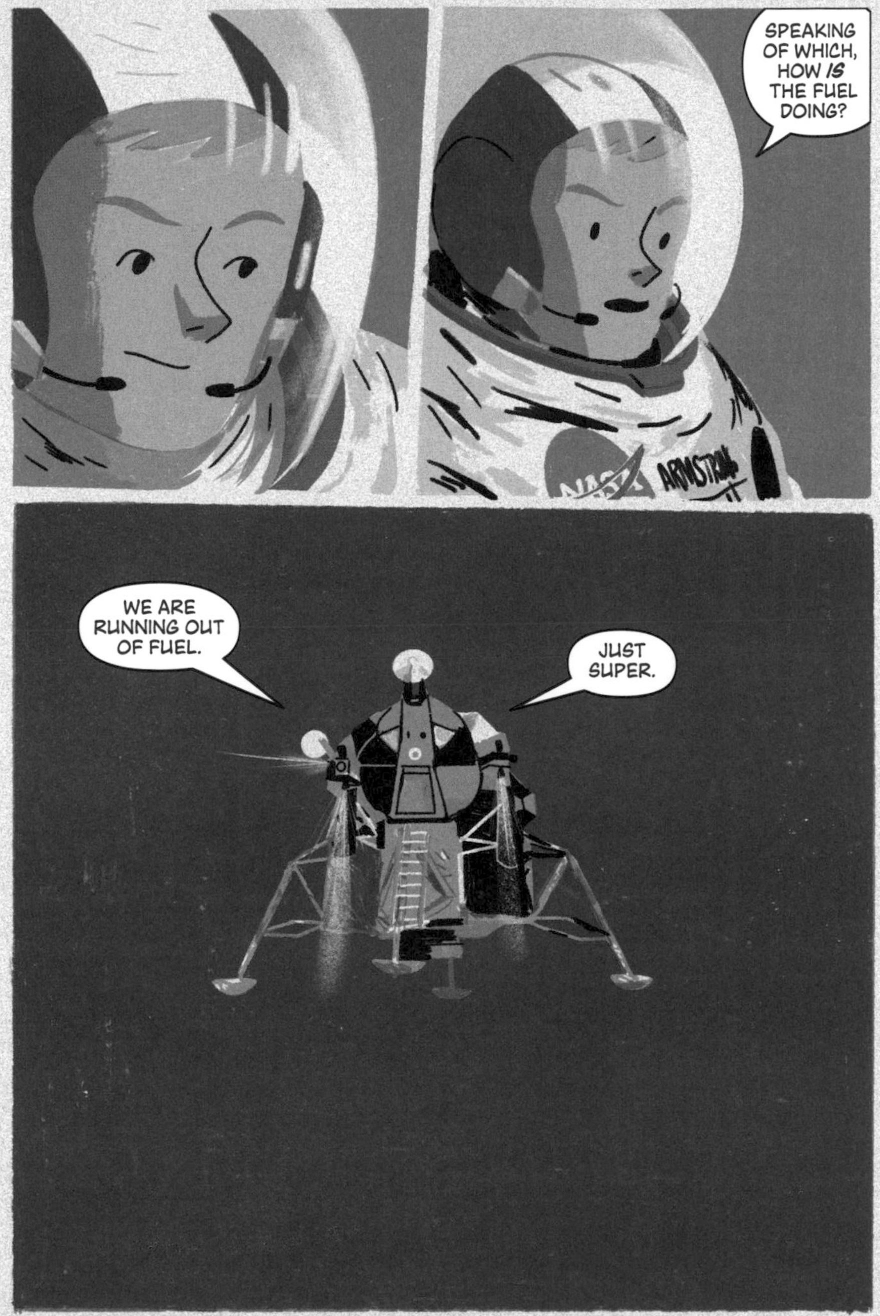
SPEAKING OF WHICH, HOW *IS* THE FUEL DOING?
WE ARE RUNNING OUT OF FUEL.
JUST SUPER.

Buzz Aldrin

Buzz Aldrin (originally Edwin Eugene Aldrin Jr.) was born January 20, 1930, and grew up in Montclair, New Jersey. He earned the nickname Buzz because his sisters, Madeline and Fay Ann, would affectionately call him "brother," but with Fay Ann just learning how to speak, it sounded like she was saying "Buzzer."

After graduating third in his class at the United States Military Academy at West Point, Buzz became an Air Force pilot in the Korean War where he flew sixty-six highly dangerous missions. He then became a NASA pilot in 1963, in the third group of men selected to be astronauts. Three years later, he established a new record at the time for extravehicular activity (spacewalking!), spending a total of five and a half hours outside of the Gemini 12 spacecraft.

After the Apollo 11 mission, Buzz was awarded the Presidential Medal of Freedom in 1969 along with the rest of the crew members. Then, in 1972, after twenty-one years of service in the Air Force, he retired from active duty and in 2011 was awarded the Congressional Gold Medal.

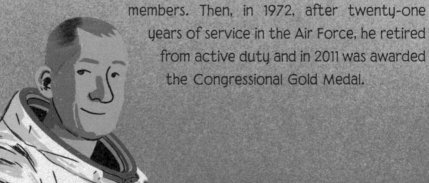

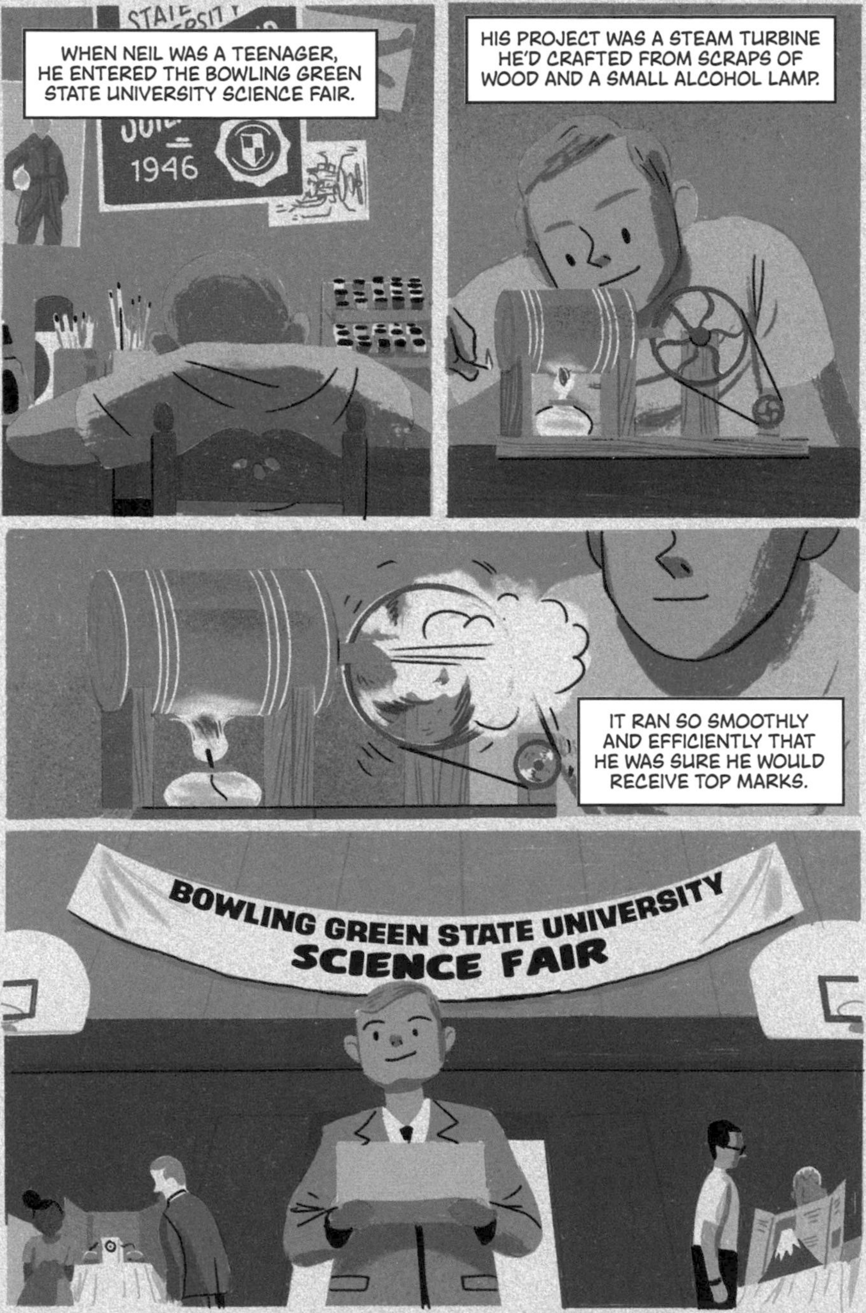
WHEN NEIL WAS A TEENAGER, HE ENTERED THE BOWLING GREEN STATE UNIVERSITY SCIENCE FAIR.
1946
HIS PROJECT WAS A STEAM TURBINE HE'D CRAFTED FROM SCRAPS OF WOOD AND A SMALL ALCOHOL LAMP.
IT RAN SO SMOOTHLY AND EFFICIENTLY THAT HE WAS SURE HE WOULD RECEIVE TOP MARKS.
BOWLING GREEN STATE UNIVERSITY
SCIENCE FAIR

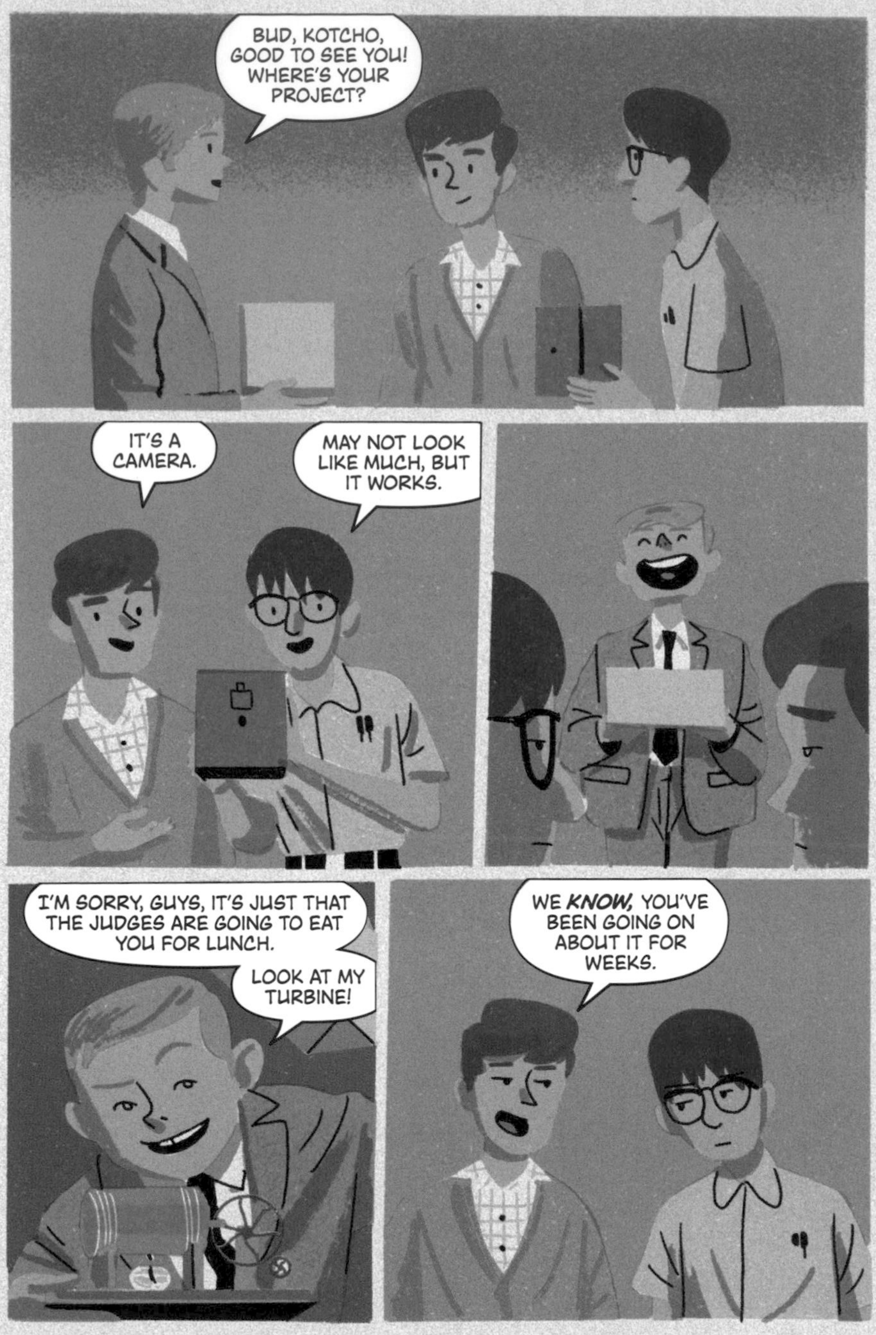
BUD, KOTCHO, GOOD TO SEE YOU! WHERE'S YOUR PROJECT?
IT'S A CAMERA.
MAY NOT LOOK LIKE MUCH, BUT IT WORKS.
I'M SORRY, GUYS, IT'S JUST THAT THE JUDGES ARE GOING TO EAT YOU FOR LUNCH.
LOOK AT MY TURBINE!
WE ***KNOW,*** YOU'VE BEEN GOING ON ABOUT IT FOR WEEKS.

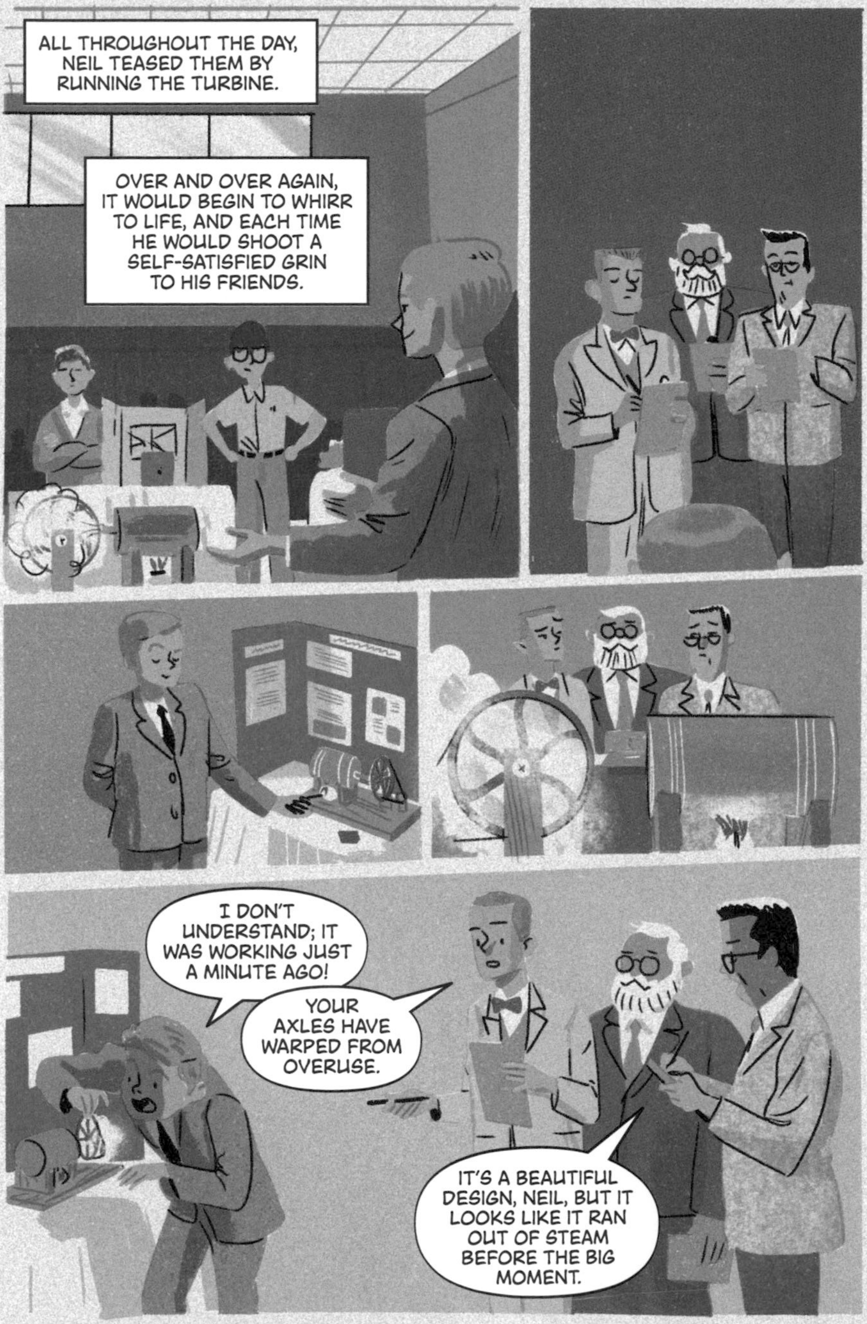
ALL THROUGHOUT THE DAY, NEIL TEASED THEM BY RUNNING THE TURBINE.
OVER AND OVER AGAIN, IT WOULD BEGIN TO WHIRR TO LIFE, AND EACH TIME HE WOULD SHOOT A SELF-SATISFIED GRIN TO HIS FRIENDS.
I DON'T UNDERSTAND; IT WAS WORKING JUST A MINUTE AGO!
YOUR AXLES HAVE WARPED FROM OVERUSE.
IT'S A BEAUTIFUL DESIGN, NEIL, BUT IT LOOKS LIKE IT RAN OUT OF STEAM BEFORE THE BIG MOMENT.

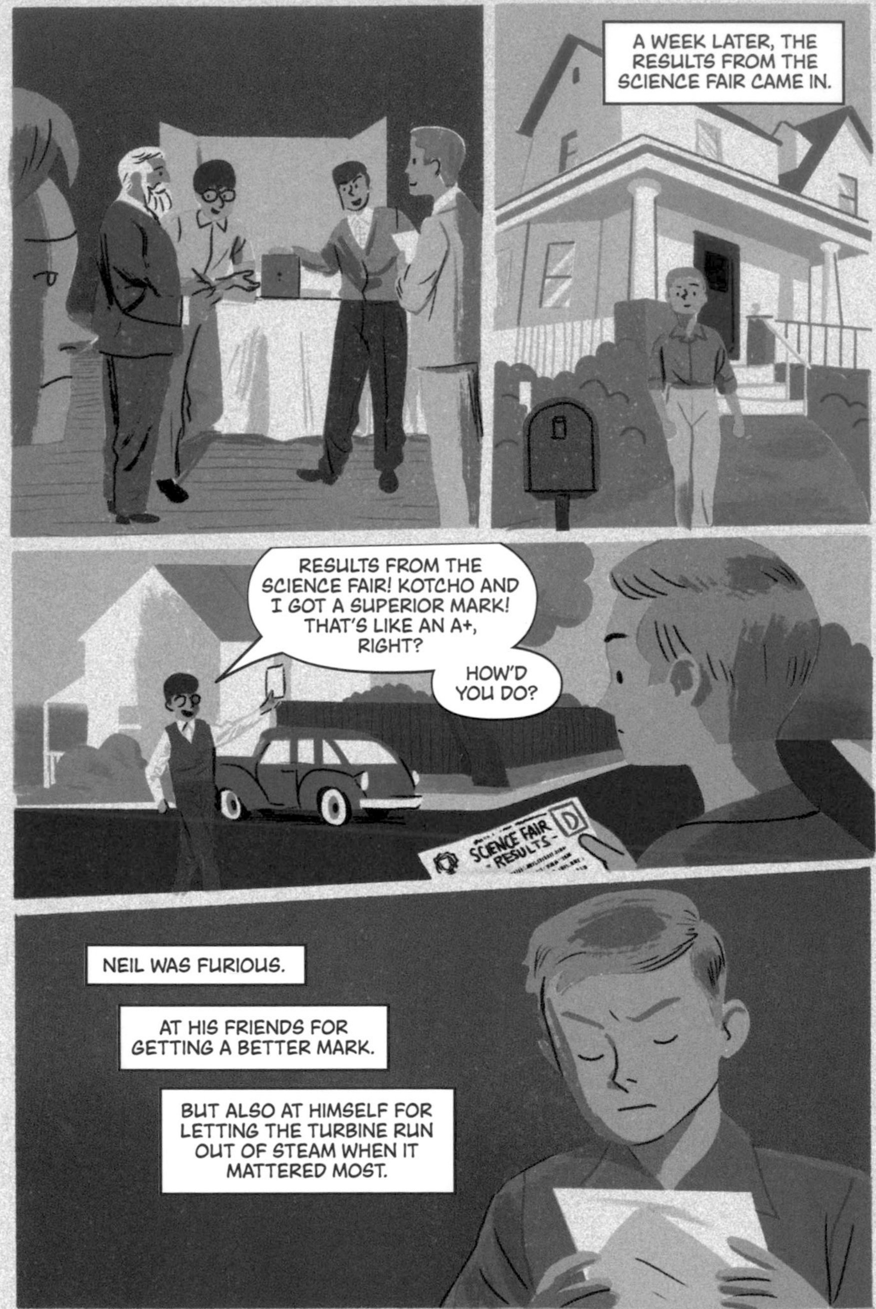
A WEEK LATER, THE RESULTS FROM THE SCIENCE FAIR CAME IN.
RESULTS FROM THE SCIENCE FAIR! KOTCHO AND I GOT A SUPERIOR MARK! THAT'S LIKE AN A+, RIGHT?
HOW'D YOU DO?
SCIENCE FAIR RESULTS
D
NEIL WAS FURIOUS.
AT HIS FRIENDS FOR GETTING A BETTER MARK.
BUT ALSO AT HIMSELF FOR LETTING THE TURBINE RUN OUT OF STEAM WHEN IT MATTERED MOST.

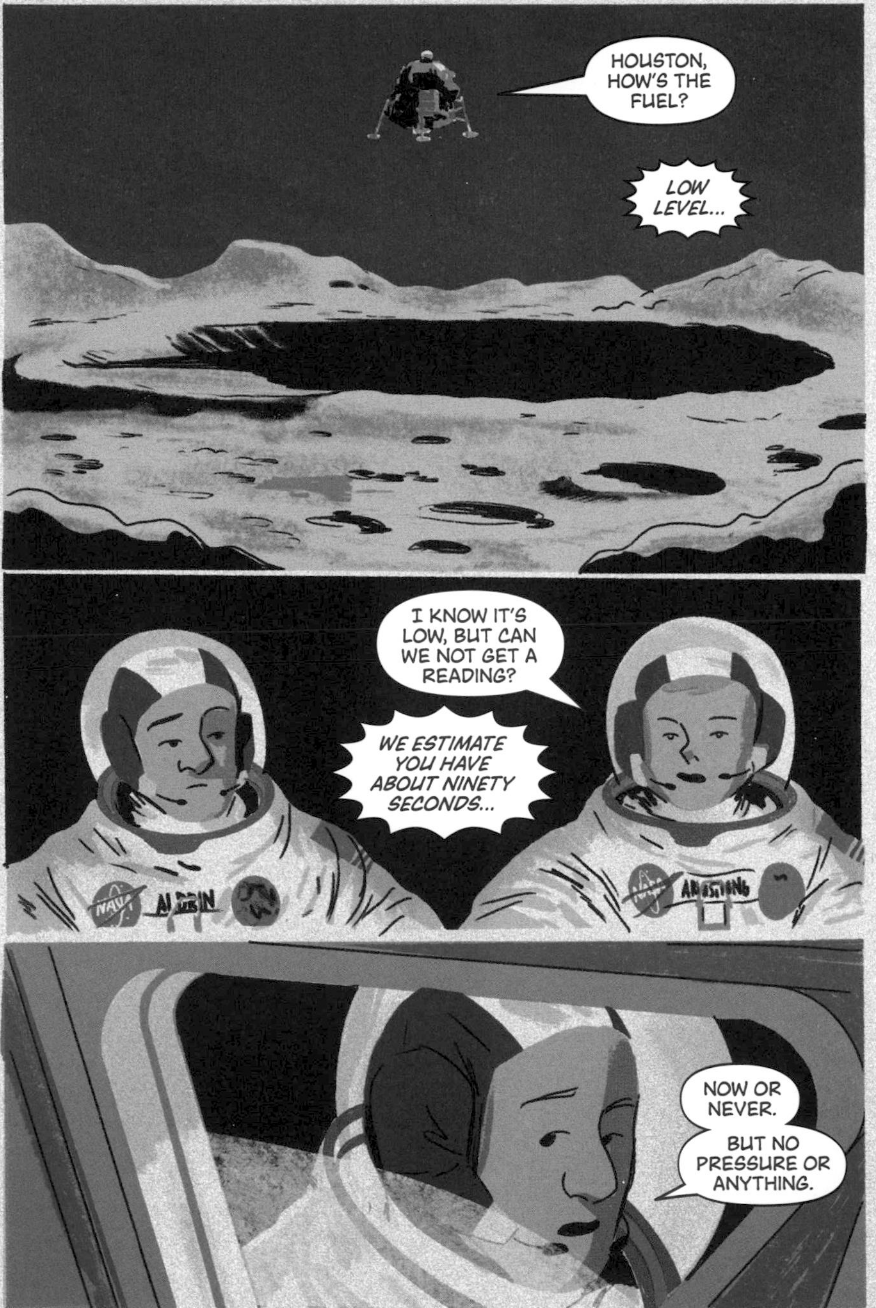
HOUSTON, HOW'S THE FUEL?
LOW LEVEL...
I KNOW IT'S LOW, BUT CAN WE NOT GET A READING?
WE ESTIMATE YOU HAVE ABOUT NINETY SECONDS...
NASA
ALDRIN
NOW OR NEVER.
BUT NO PRESSURE OR ANYTHING.

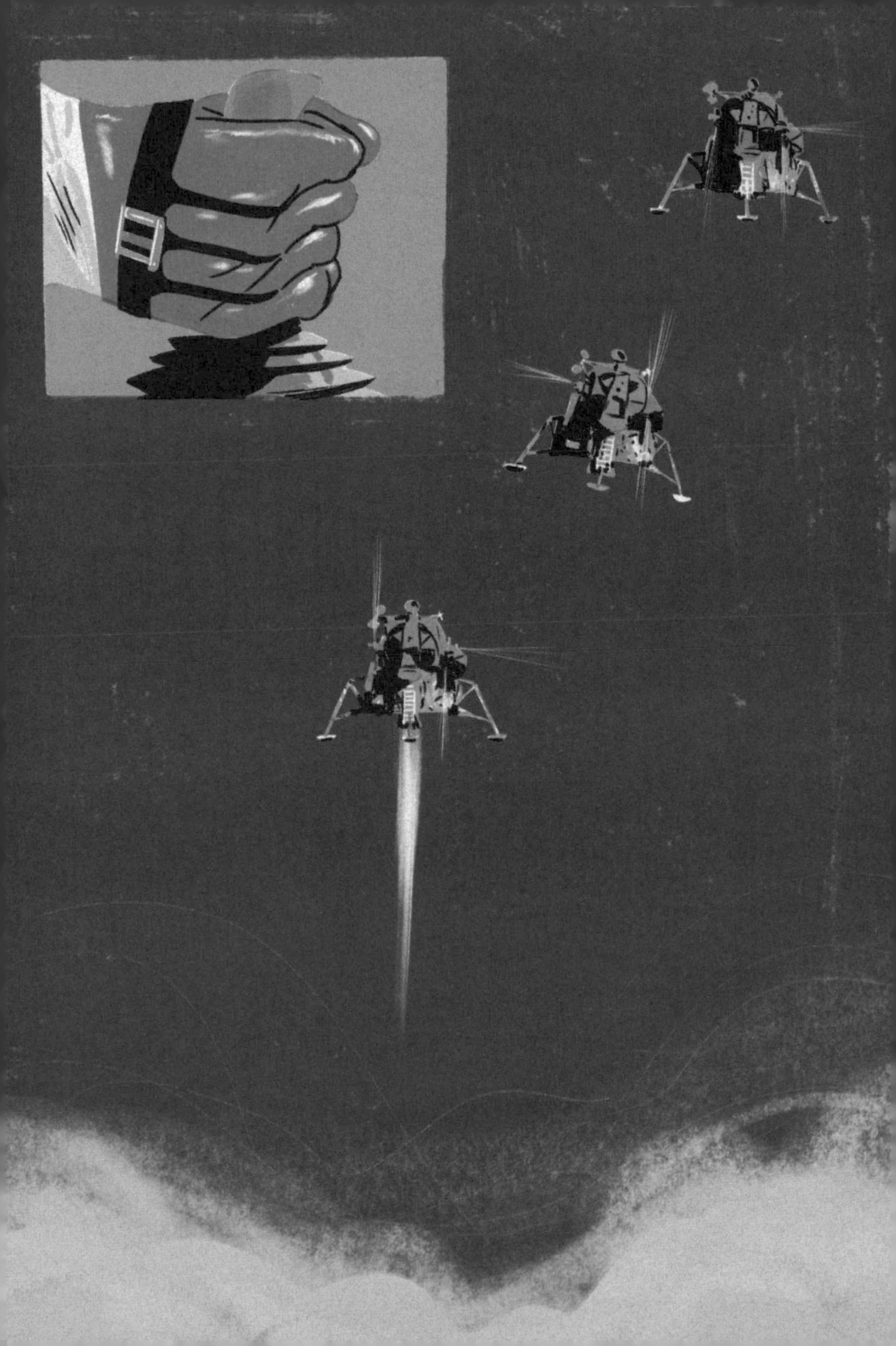

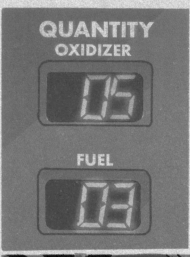

QUANTITY
OXIDIZER

05

FUEL

03

QUANTITY LIGHT. THAT PUTS US AT LESS THAN 5 PERCENT FUEL REMAINING AND GIVES US ABOUT...

SIXTY SECONDS BEFORE WE HAVE TO CALL ABORT, GENTLEMEN.

WE AREN'T GOING BACK. WE ARE LANDING ON THE MOON *TODAY.*

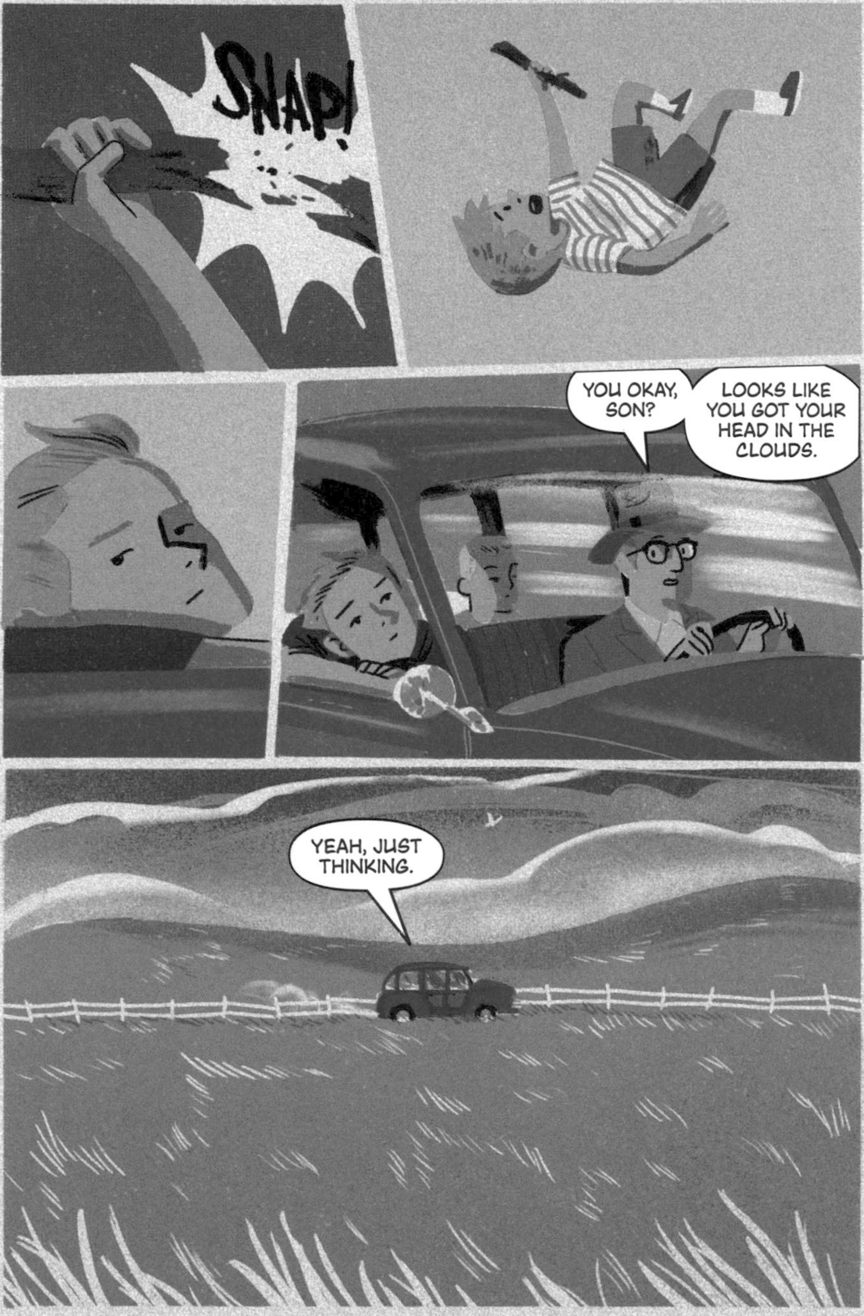
SNAP!
YOU OKAY, SON?
LOOKS LIKE YOU GOT YOUR HEAD IN THE CLOUDS.
YEAH, JUST THINKING.

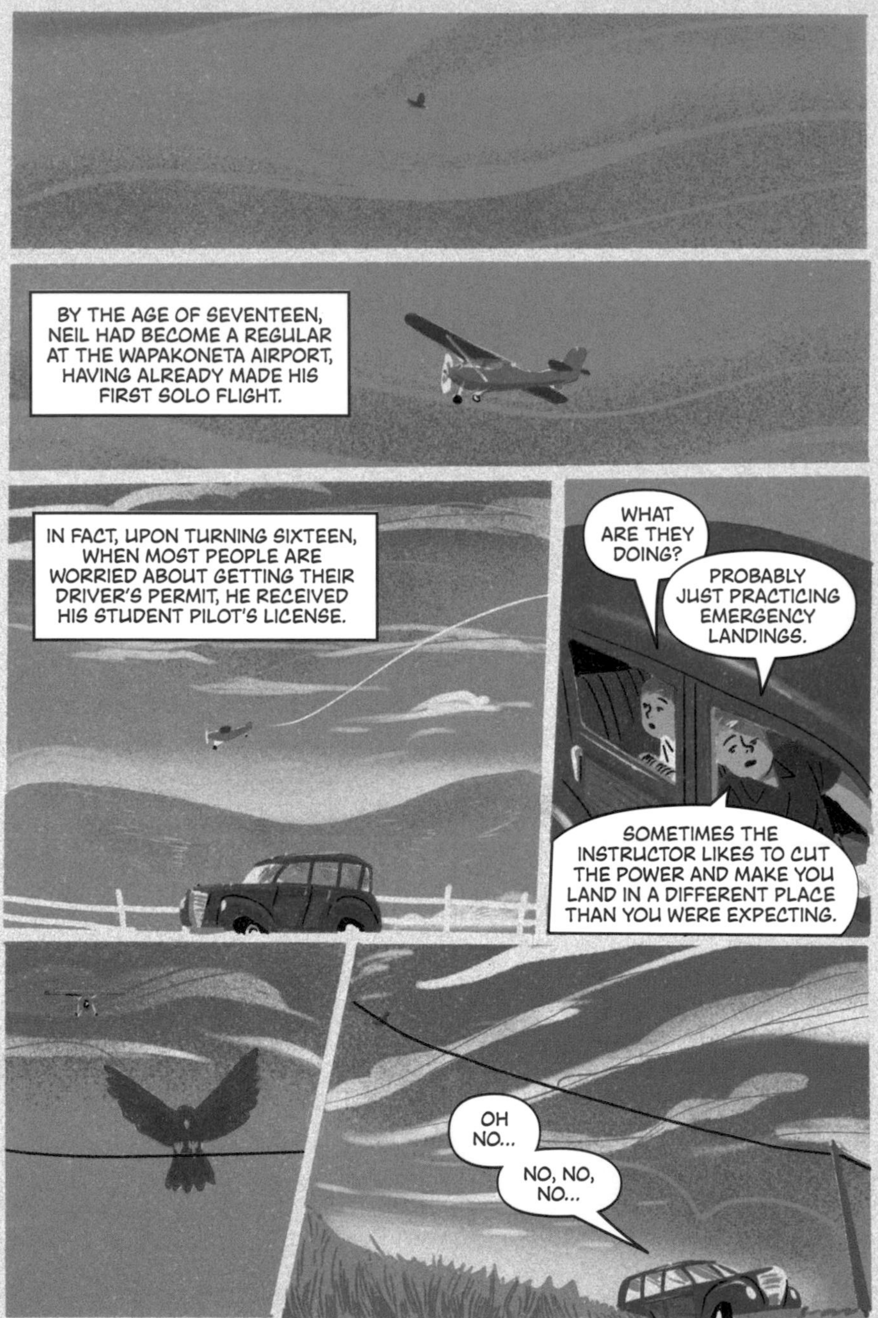
BY THE AGE OF SEVENTEEN, NEIL HAD BECOME A REGULAR AT THE WAPAKONETA AIRPORT, HAVING ALREADY MADE HIS FIRST SOLO FLIGHT.
IN FACT, UPON TURNING SIXTEEN, WHEN MOST PEOPLE ARE WORRIED ABOUT GETTING THEIR DRIVER'S PERMIT, HE RECEIVED HIS STUDENT PILOT'S LICENSE.
WHAT ARE THEY DOING?
PROBABLY JUST PRACTICING EMERGENCY LANDINGS.
SOMETIMES THE INSTRUCTOR LIKES TO CUT THE POWER AND MAKE YOU LAND IN A DIFFERENT PLACE THAN YOU WERE EXPECTING.
OH NO...
NO, NO, NO...

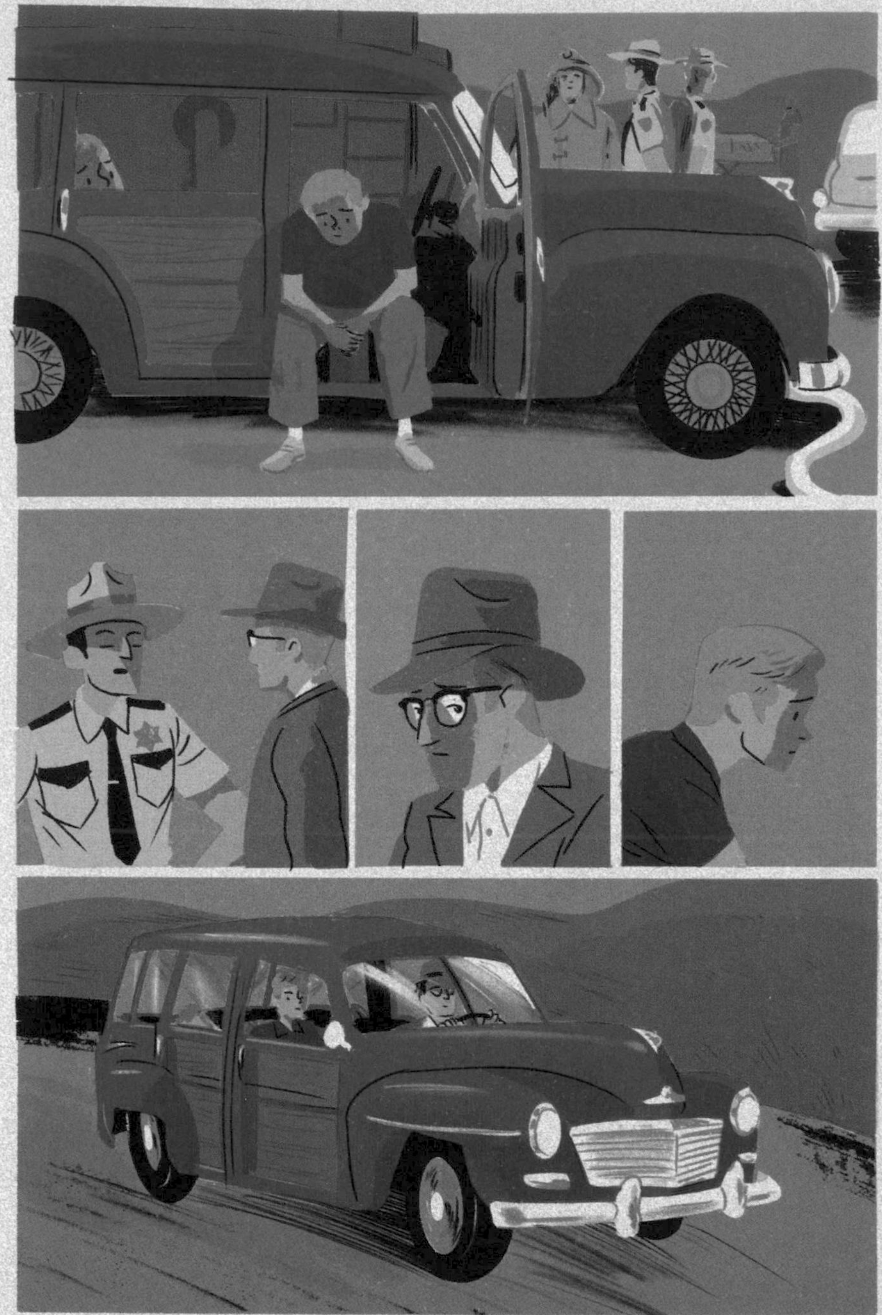

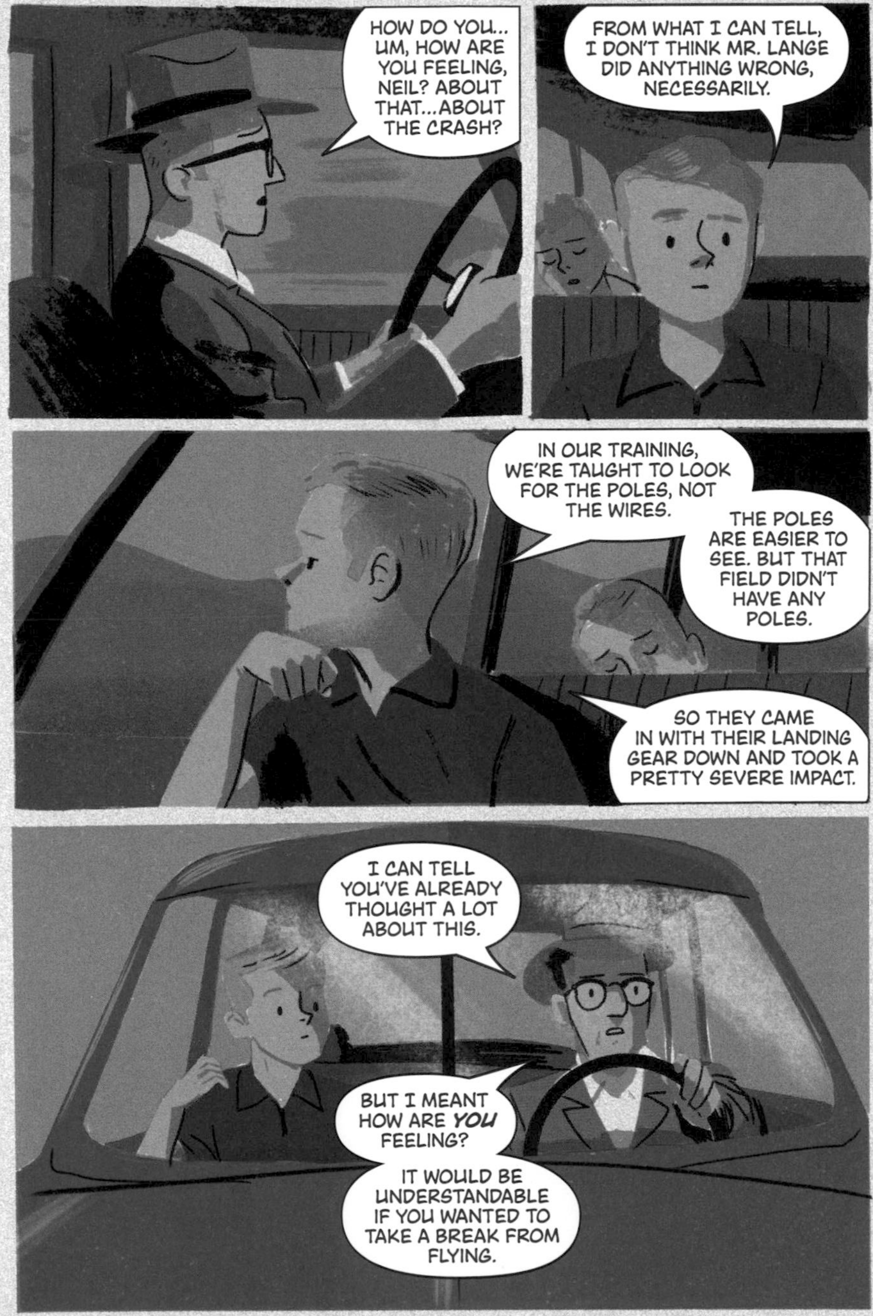
HOW DO YOU... UM, HOW ARE YOU FEELING, NEIL? ABOUT THAT...ABOUT THE CRASH?
FROM WHAT I CAN TELL, I DON'T THINK MR. LANGE DID ANYTHING WRONG, NECESSARILY.
IN OUR TRAINING, WE'RE TAUGHT TO LOOK FOR THE POLES, NOT THE WIRES.
THE POLES ARE EASIER TO SEE. BUT THAT FIELD DIDN'T HAVE ANY POLES.
SO THEY CAME IN WITH THEIR LANDING GEAR DOWN AND TOOK A PRETTY SEVERE IMPACT.
I CAN TELL YOU'VE ALREADY THOUGHT A LOT ABOUT THIS.
BUT I MEANT HOW ARE *YOU* FEELING?
IT WOULD BE UNDERSTANDABLE IF YOU WANTED TO TAKE A BREAK FROM FLYING.

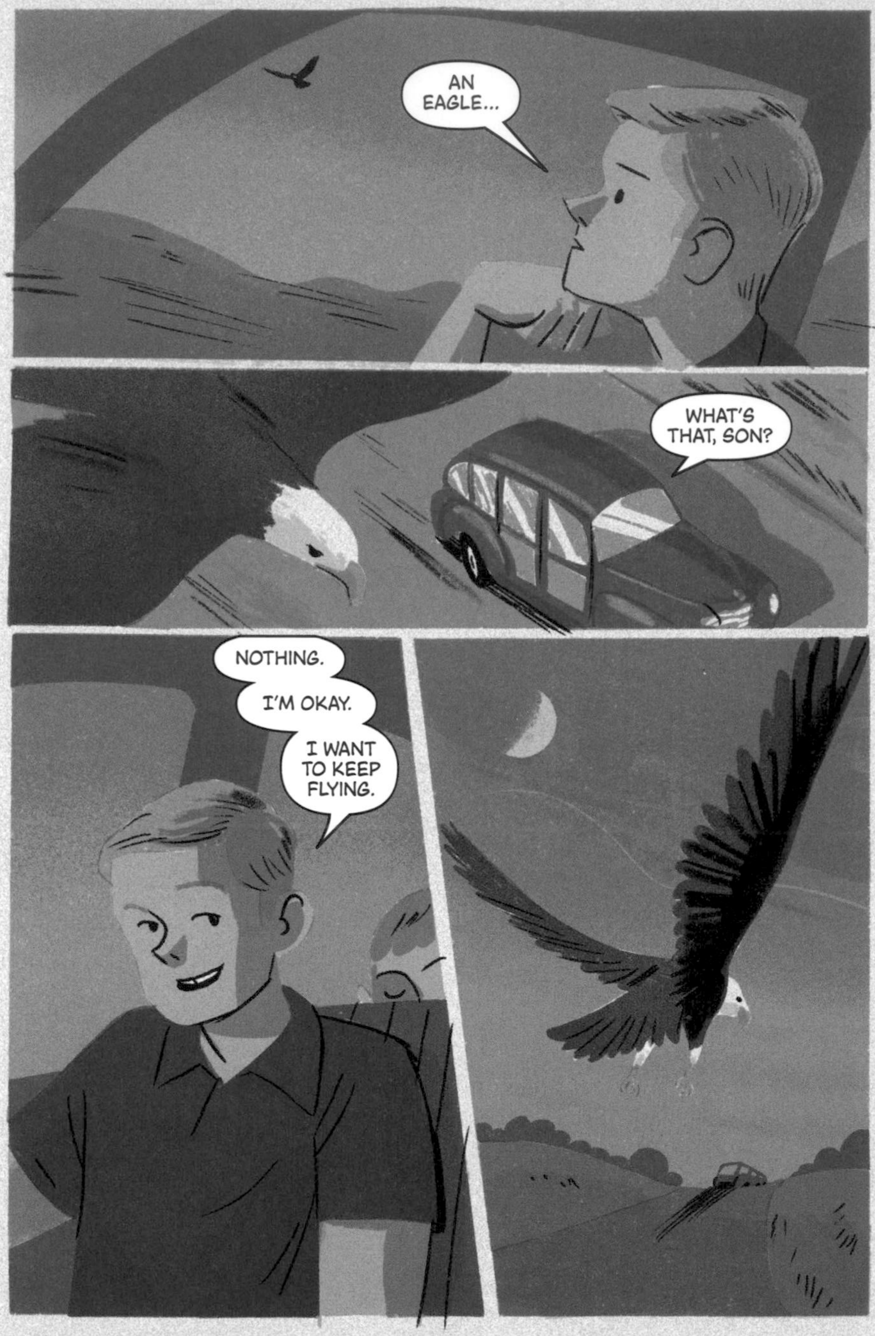
AN EAGLE...
WHAT'S THAT, SON?
NOTHING.
I'M OKAY.
I WANT TO KEEP FLYING.

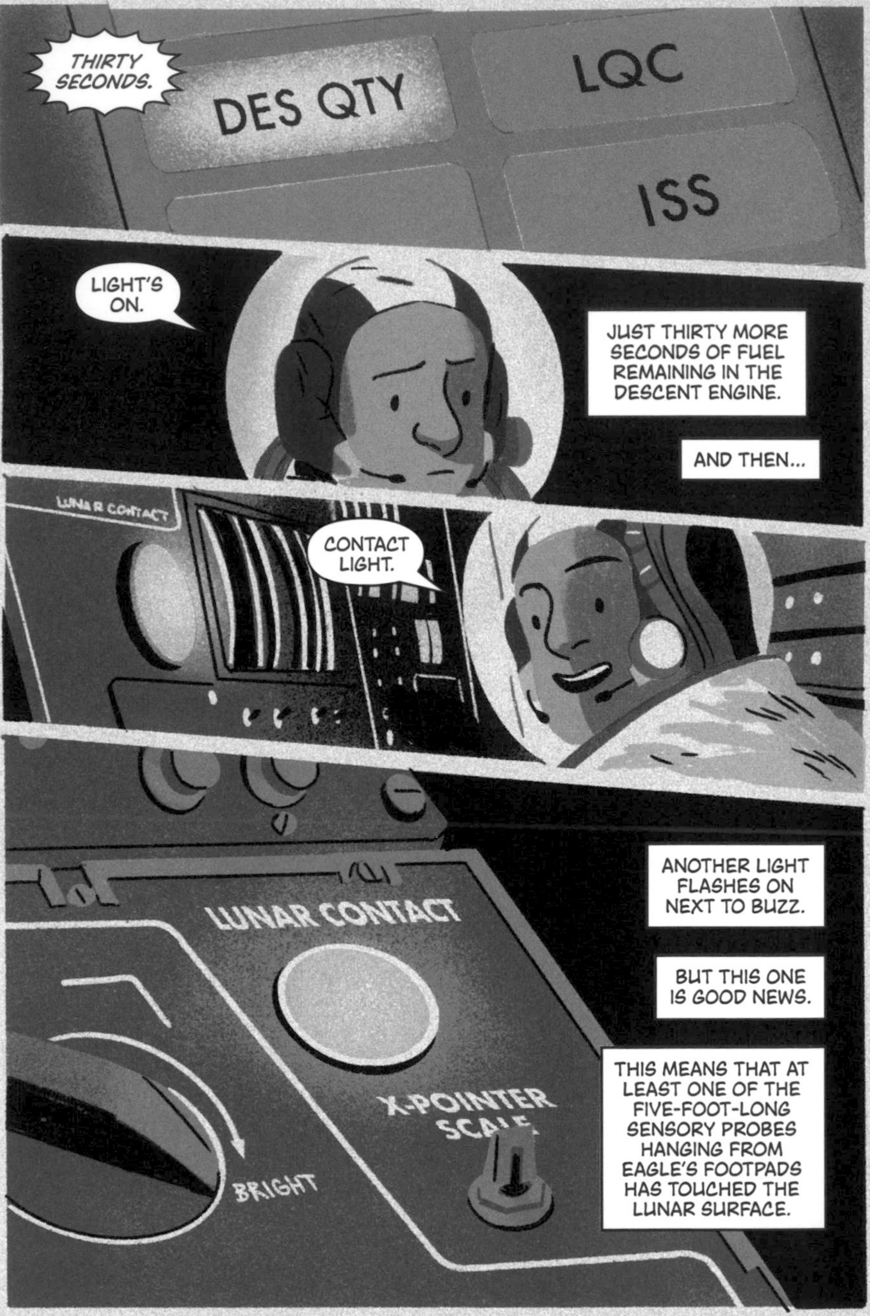
THIRTY SECONDS.
DES QTY
LQC
ISS
LIGHT'S ON.
JUST THIRTY MORE SECONDS OF FUEL REMAINING IN THE DESCENT ENGINE.
AND THEN...
LUNAR CONTACT
CONTACT LIGHT.
ANOTHER LIGHT FLASHES ON NEXT TO BUZZ.
BUT THIS ONE IS GOOD NEWS.
LUNAR CONTACT
THIS MEANS THAT AT LEAST ONE OF THE FIVE-FOOT-LONG SENSORY PROBES HANGING FROM EAGLE'S FOOTPADS HAS TOUCHED THE LUNAR SURFACE.
X-POINTER
BRIGHT

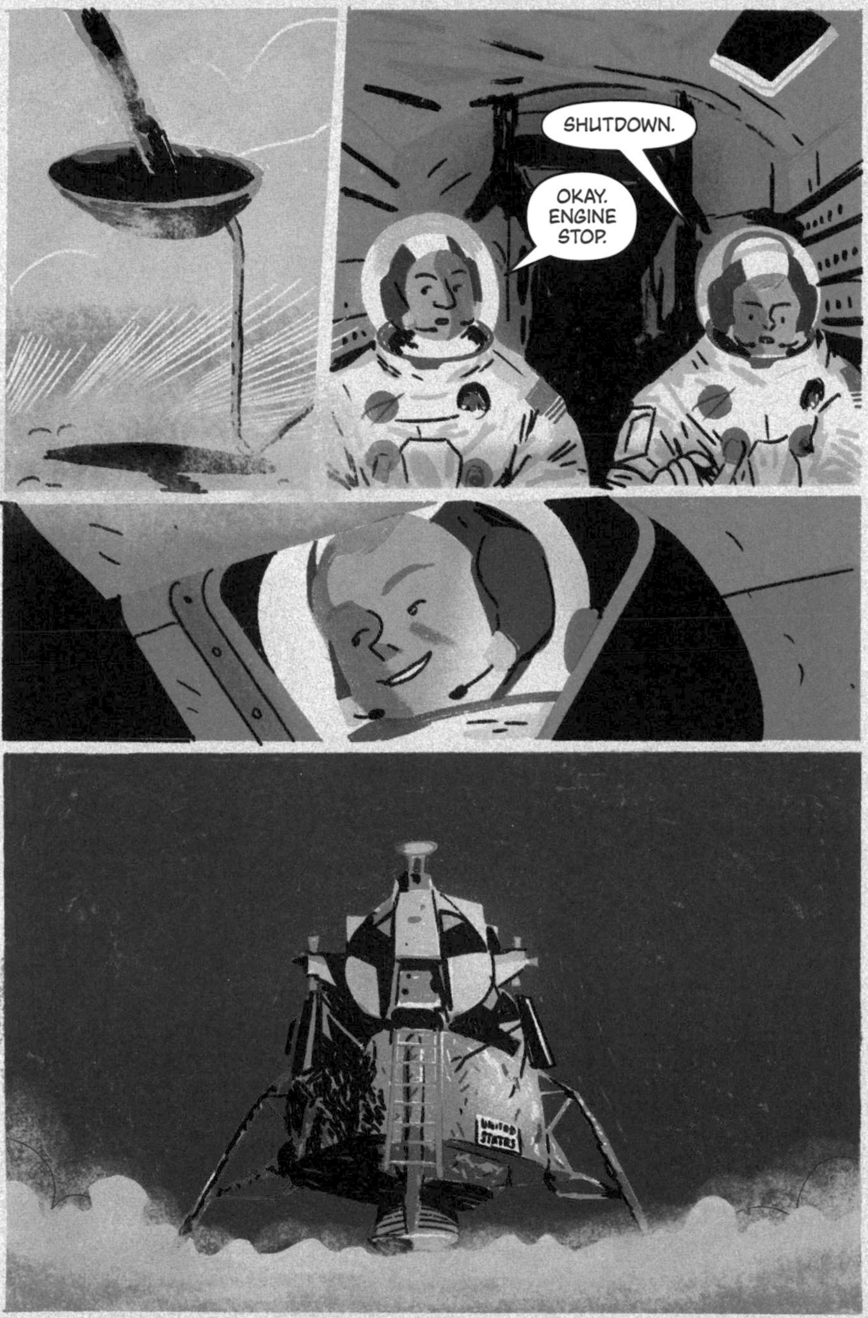
SHUTDOWN.
OKAY. ENGINE STOP.
UNITED STATES

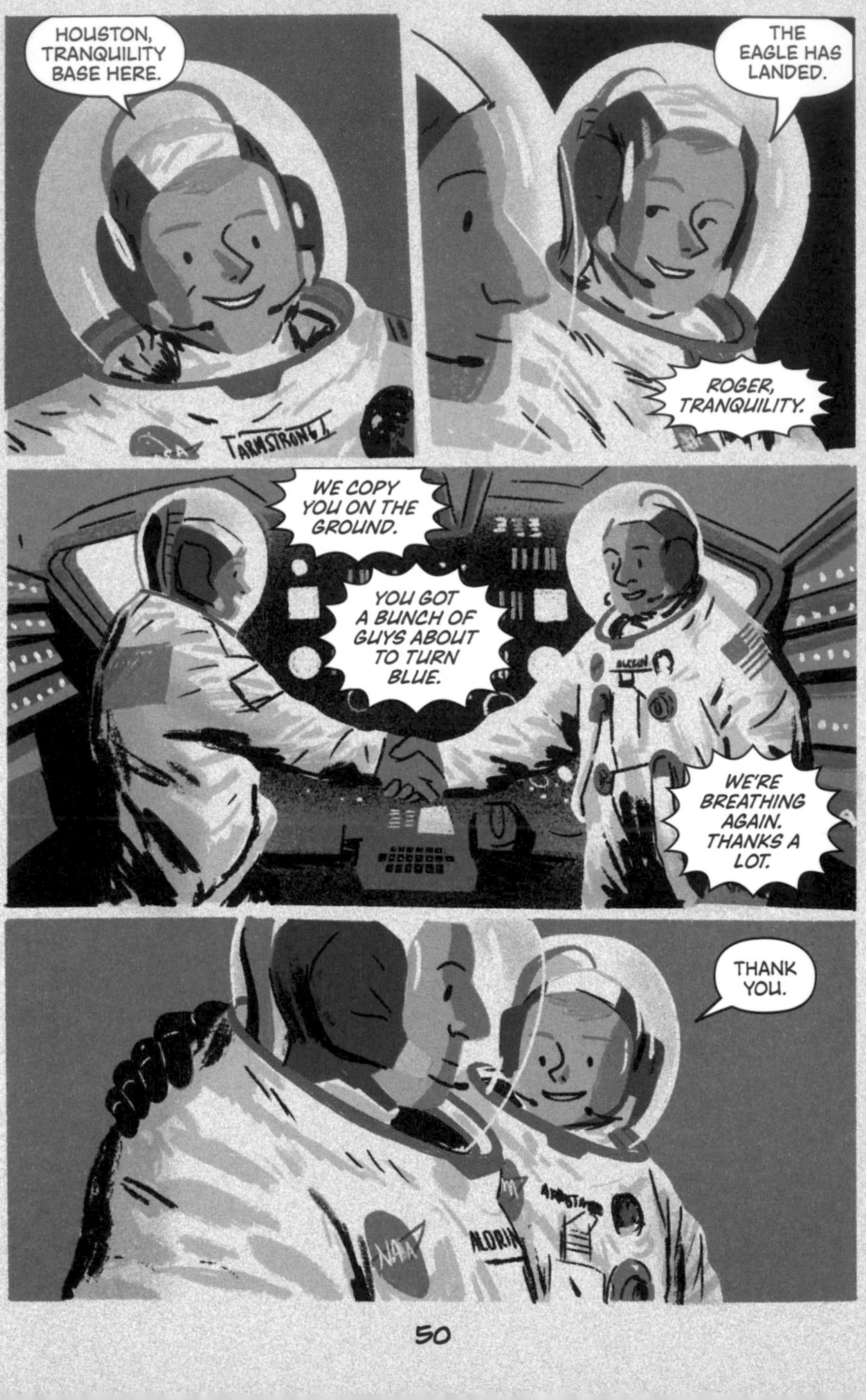
HOUSTON, TRANQUILITY BASE HERE.
THE EAGLE HAS LANDED.
ROGER, TRANQUILITY.
WE COPY YOU ON THE GROUND.
YOU GOT A BUNCH OF GUYS ABOUT TO TURN BLUE.
WE'RE BREATHING AGAIN. THANKS A LOT.
THANK YOU.

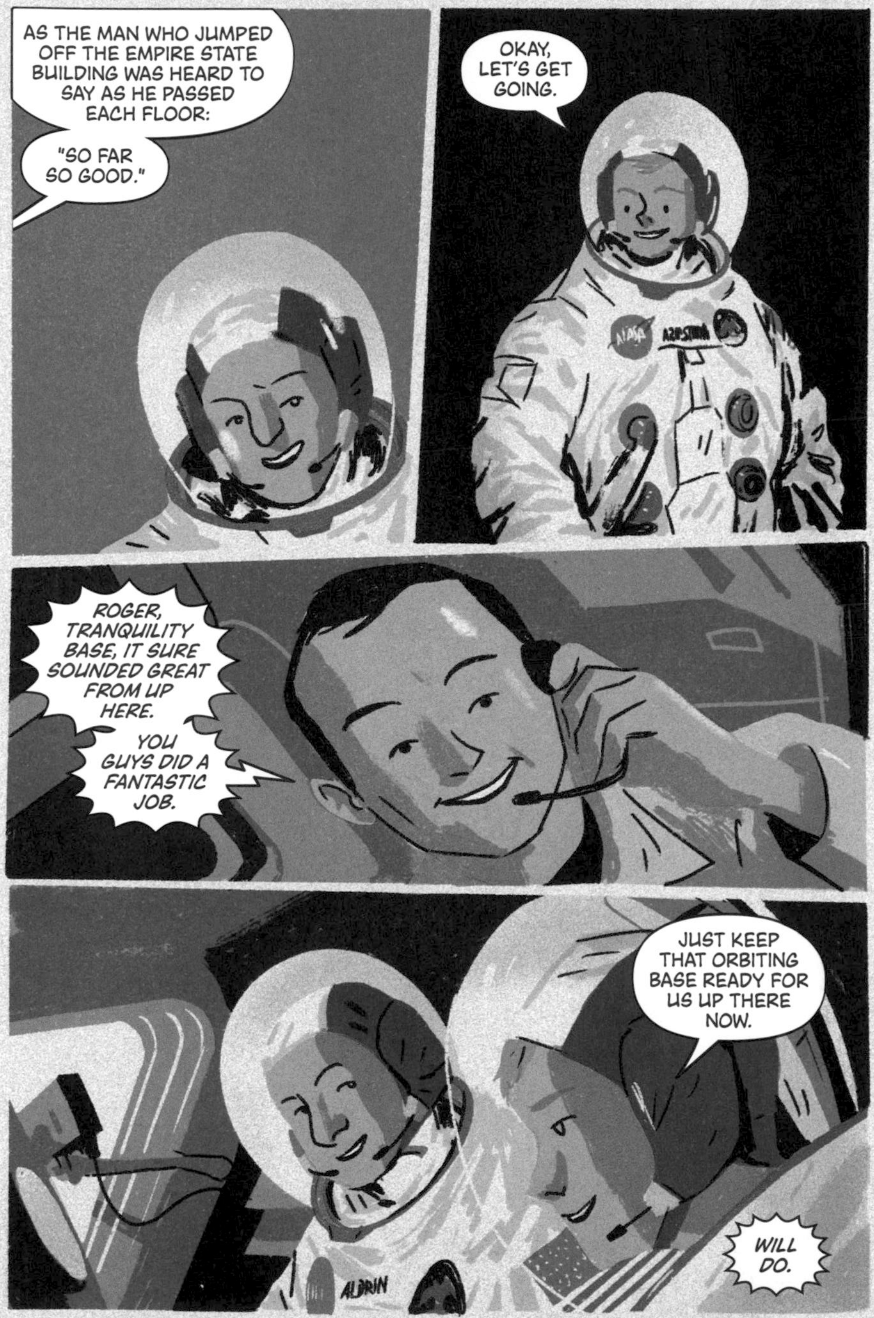
AS THE MAN WHO JUMPED OFF THE EMPIRE STATE BUILDING WAS HEARD TO SAY AS HE PASSED EACH FLOOR:
"SO FAR SO GOOD."
OKAY, LET'S GET GOING.
NASA
ROGER, TRANQUILITY BASE, IT SURE SOUNDED GREAT FROM UP HERE.
YOU GUYS DID A FANTASTIC JOB.
JUST KEEP THAT ORBITING BASE READY FOR US UP THERE NOW.
WILL DO.
ALDRIN

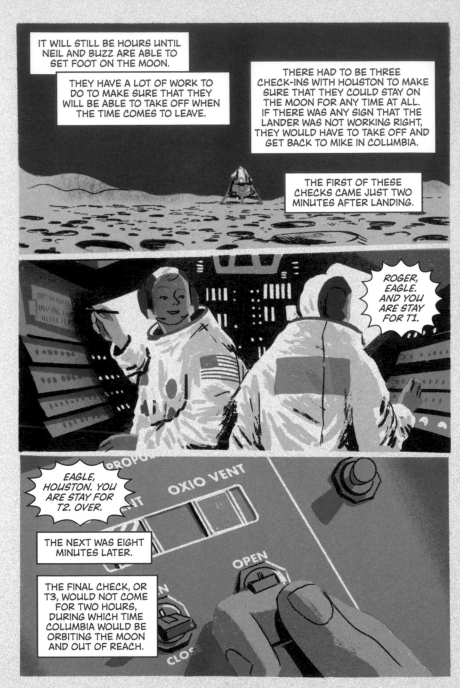

IT WILL STILL BE HOURS UNTIL NEIL AND BUZZ ARE ABLE TO SET FOOT ON THE MOON.

THEY HAVE A LOT OF WORK TO DO TO MAKE SURE THAT THEY WILL BE ABLE TO TAKE OFF WHEN THE TIME COMES TO LEAVE.

THERE HAD TO BE THREE CHECK-INS WITH HOUSTON TO MAKE SURE THAT THEY COULD STAY ON THE MOON FOR ANY TIME AT ALL. IF THERE WAS ANY SIGN THAT THE LANDER WAS NOT WORKING RIGHT, THEY WOULD HAVE TO TAKE OFF AND GET BACK TO MIKE IN COLUMBIA.

THE FIRST OF THESE CHECKS CAME JUST TWO MINUTES AFTER LANDING.

ROGER, EAGLE. AND YOU ARE STAY FOR T1.

EAGLE, HOUSTON. YOU ARE STAY FOR T2. OVER.

THE NEXT WAS EIGHT MINUTES LATER.

THE FINAL CHECK, OR T3, WOULD NOT COME FOR TWO HOURS, DURING WHICH TIME COLUMBIA WOULD BE ORBITING THE MOON AND OUT OF REACH.

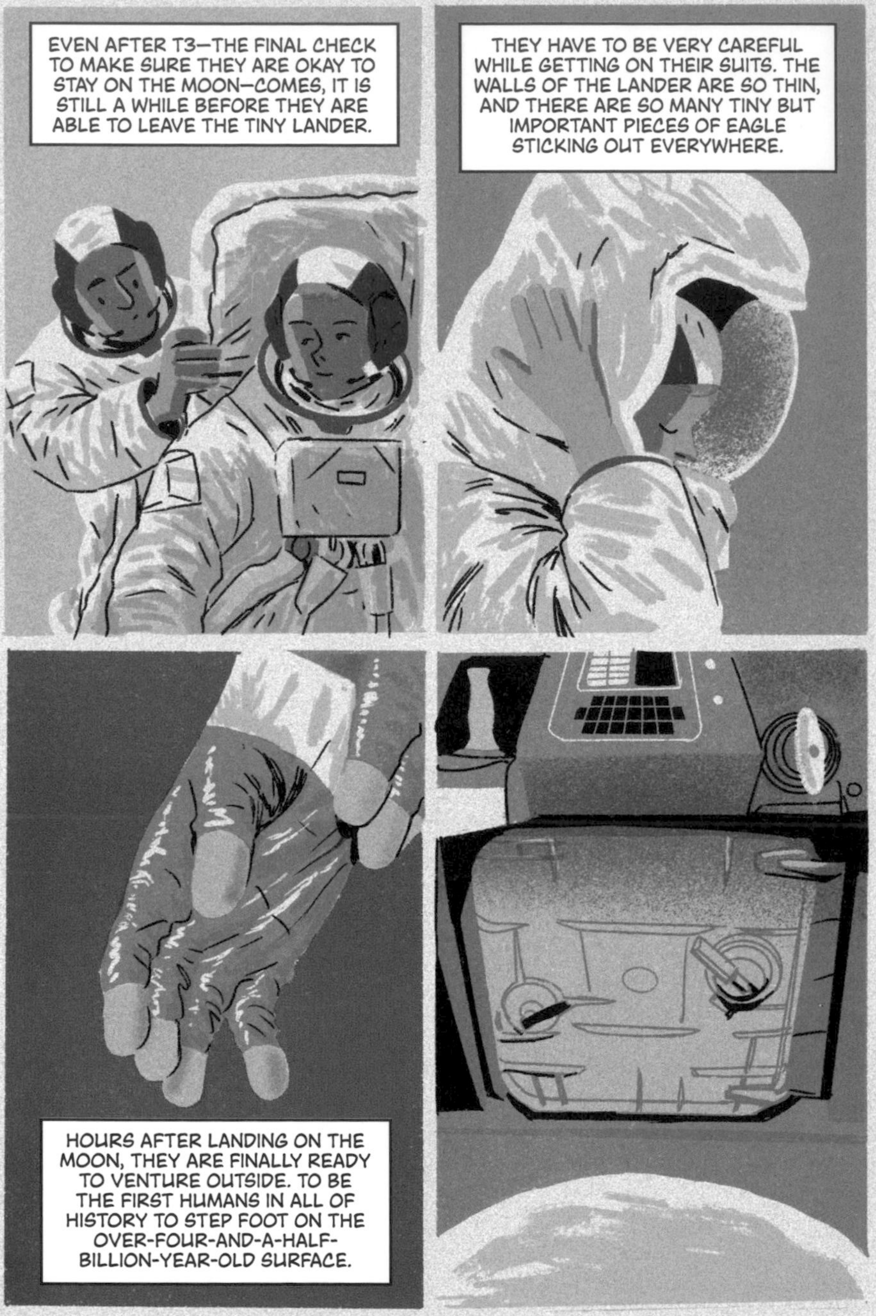

EVEN AFTER T3—THE FINAL CHECK TO MAKE SURE THEY ARE OKAY TO STAY ON THE MOON—COMES, IT IS STILL A WHILE BEFORE THEY ARE ABLE TO LEAVE THE TINY LANDER.
THEY HAVE TO BE VERY CAREFUL WHILE GETTING ON THEIR SUITS. THE WALLS OF THE LANDER ARE SO THIN, AND THERE ARE SO MANY TINY BUT IMPORTANT PIECES OF EAGLE STICKING OUT EVERYWHERE.
HOURS AFTER LANDING ON THE MOON, THEY ARE FINALLY READY TO VENTURE OUTSIDE. TO BE THE FIRST HUMANS IN ALL OF HISTORY TO STEP FOOT ON THE OVER-FOUR-AND-A-HALF-BILLION-YEAR-OLD SURFACE.

NASA Space Suit

One of the many things scientists at NASA had to figure out before going into space, let alone landing on the moon, was how the astronauts could survive without any air. This is why in every picture of an astronaut on a mission, they are wearing those oversize suits.

These are called pressure suits, or extravehicular mobility units (EMUs), and they provide the external pressure the astronauts need in order to make their lungs draw in breath when they are outside of the spacecraft.

Before getting into the suits, however, the astronauts had to put on a cooling unit, which circulates cool water in order to keep body temperatures down when wearing the airtight suits. Other elements of the suit included thick boots that were able to withstand temperatures from 250 degrees above zero to 250 degrees below; gloves covered with a fine metal mesh to prevent the more vulnerable layers from cuts and tears; a "Snoopy cap" which was a soft hood that had earphones and a microphone; and a helmet shaped like a big goldfish bowl, with a two-layered shield coated in gold to protect the astronauts from the dangerous rays of the sun.

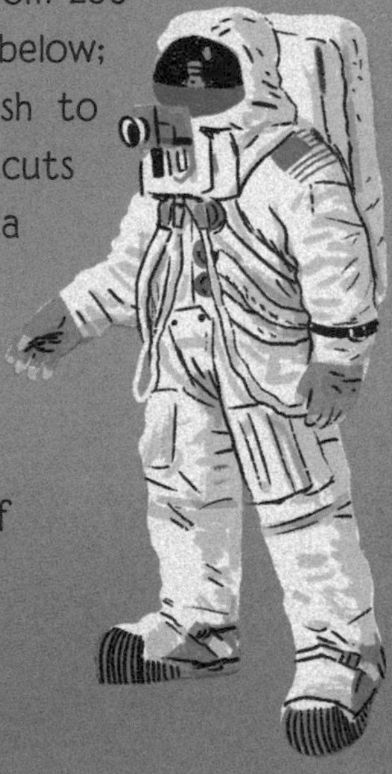

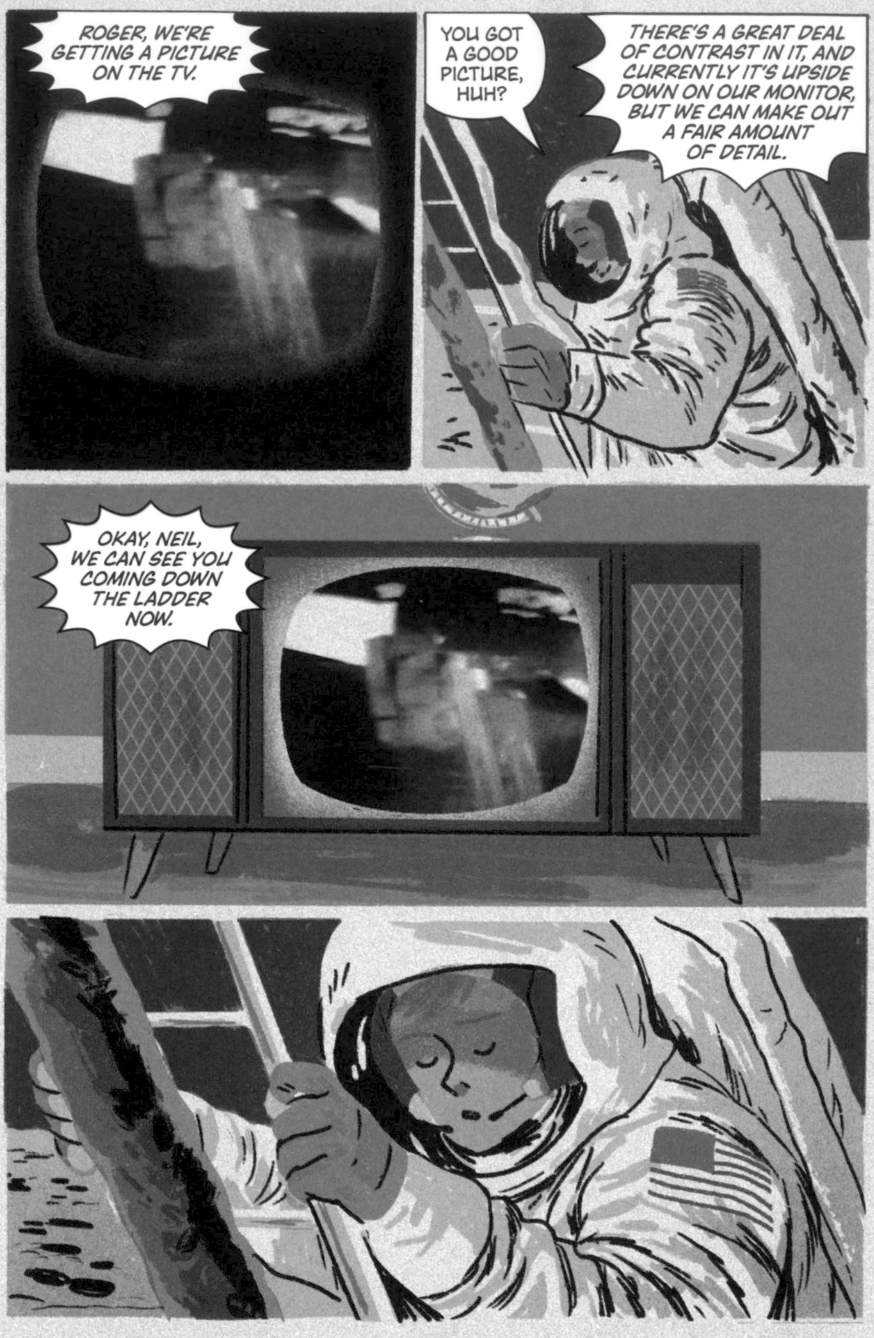
ROGER, WE'RE GETTING A PICTURE ON THE TV.
YOU GOT A GOOD PICTURE, HUH?
THERE'S A GREAT DEAL OF CONTRAST IN IT, AND CURRENTLY IT'S UPSIDE DOWN ON OUR MONITOR, BUT WE CAN MAKE OUT A FAIR AMOUNT OF DETAIL.
OKAY, NEIL, WE CAN SEE YOU COMING DOWN THE LADDER NOW.

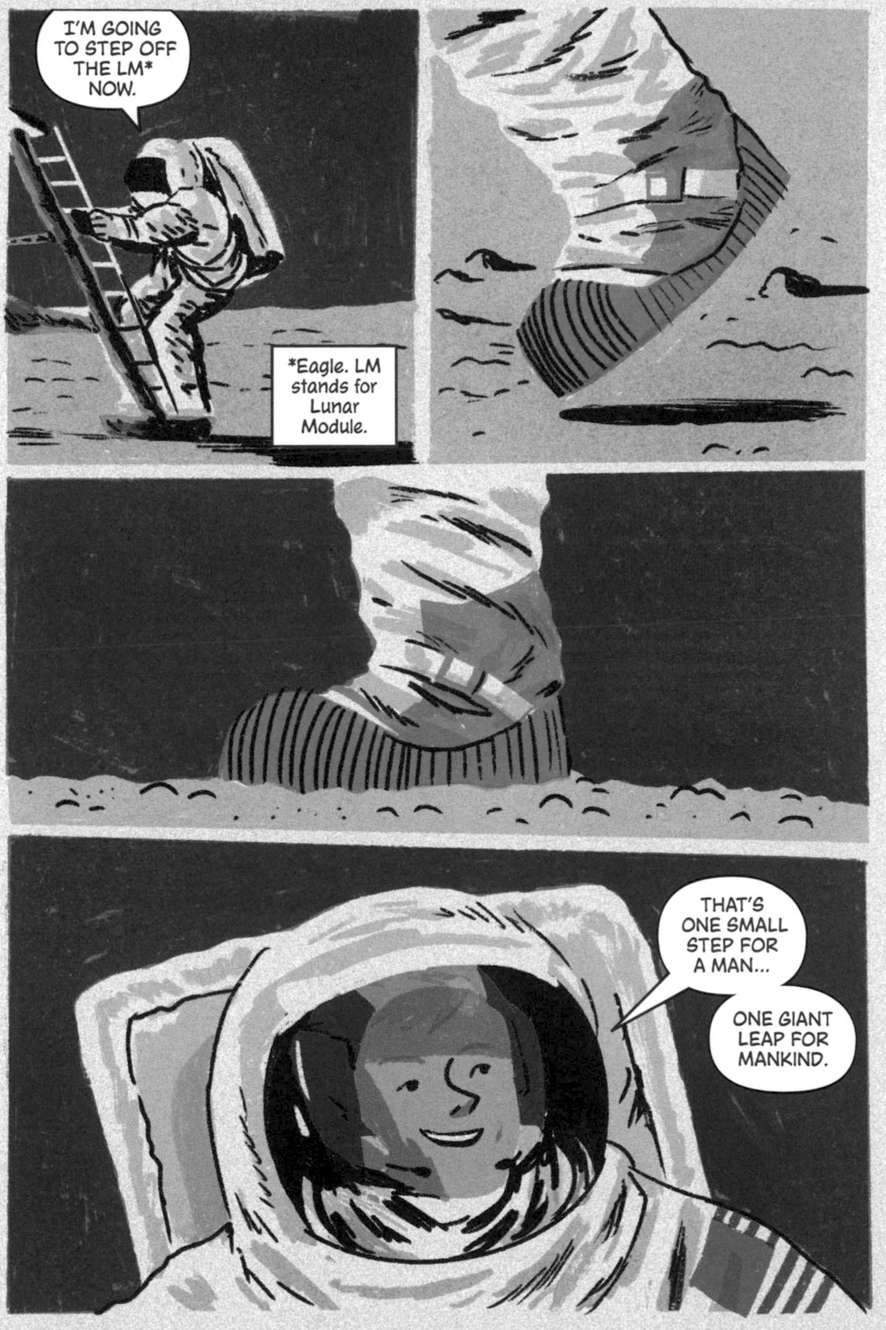

I'M GOING TO STEP OFF THE LM* NOW.
*Eagle. LM stands for Lunar Module.
THAT'S ONE SMALL STEP FOR A MAN...
ONE GIANT LEAP FOR MANKIND.

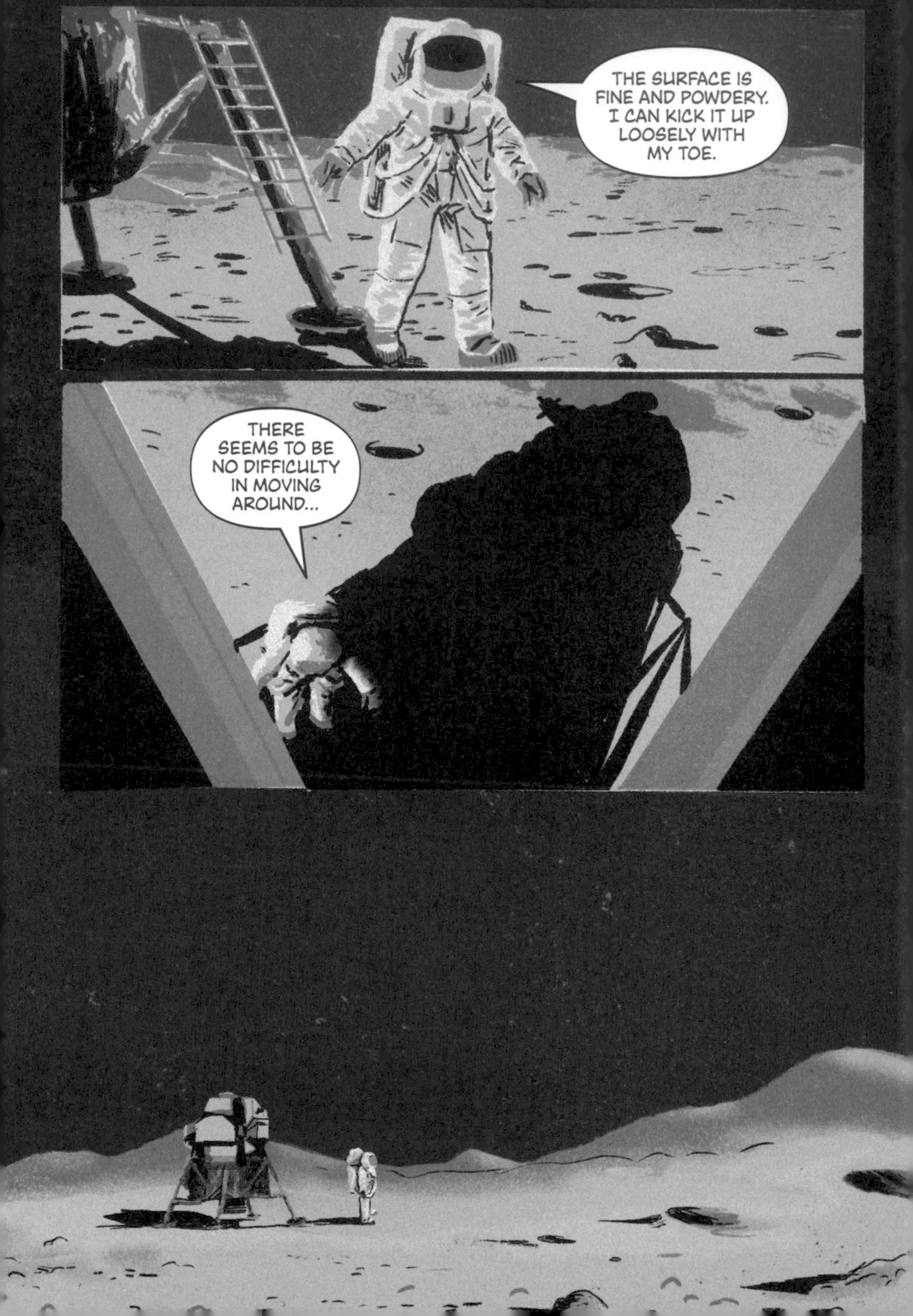
THE SURFACE IS FINE AND POWDERY. I CAN KICK IT UP LOOSELY WITH MY TOE.
THERE SEEMS TO BE NO DIFFICULTY IN MOVING AROUND...

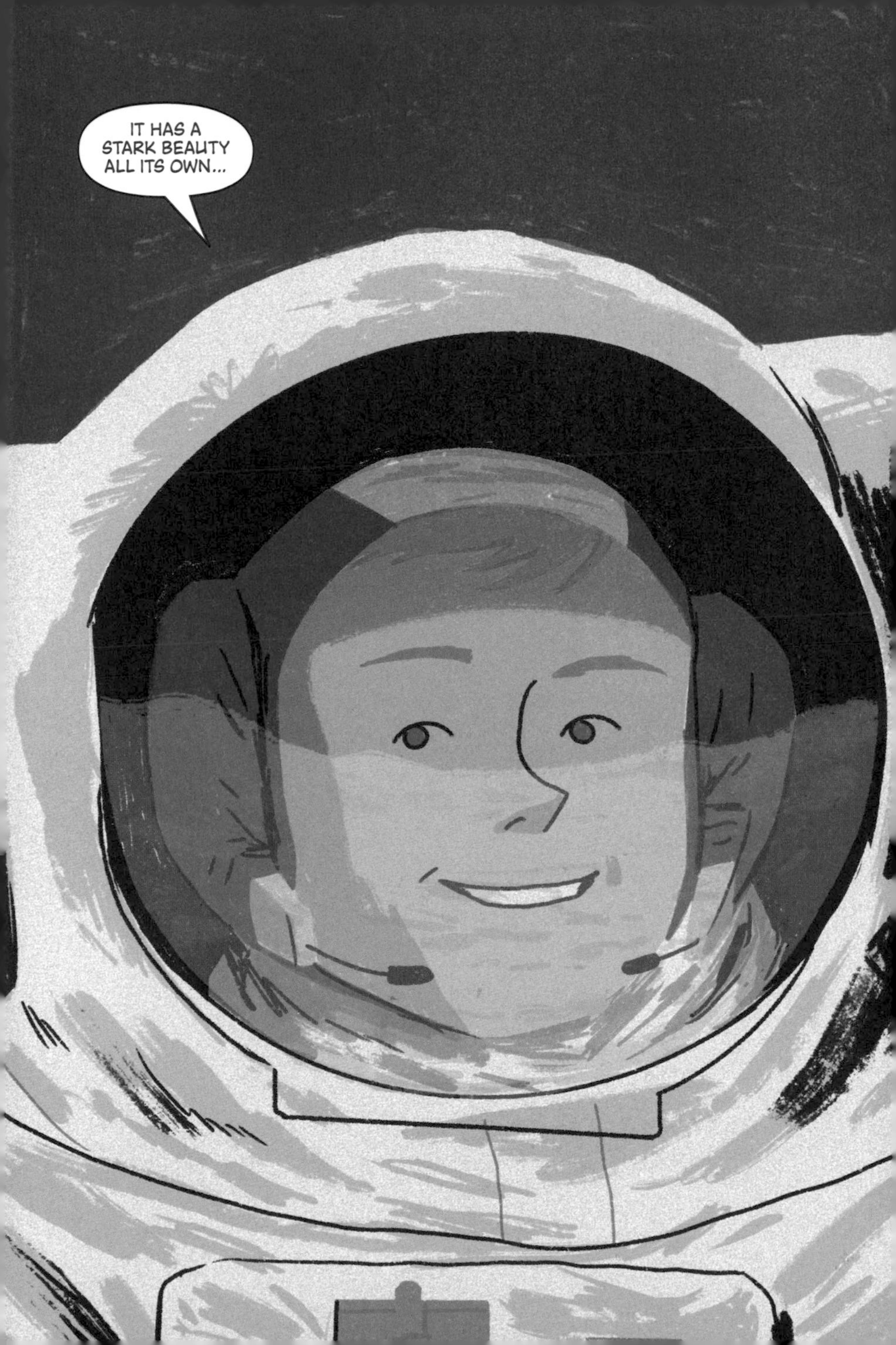
IT HAS A STARK BEAUTY ALL ITS OWN...

Conclusion

Neil Armstrong's journey to the moon began long before Apollo 11, Gemini 8, or even being named an astronaut. It started in a small Ohio town in the 1930s, where, as a young boy, Neil's dream of a life of flying became a reality, and he learned the lessons that would mold him into the person we celebrate today. The first man to walk on the moon.

Like Mike and Buzz, Neil was also the recipient of the Presidential Medal of Freedom in 1969 and the Congressional Gold Medal in 2011, as well as many other awards and honors. After retiring from NASA, Neil was a professor at the University of Cincinnati from 1971 to 1979, teaching engineering courses in aircraft design and experimental flight.

In 2011, at the age of eighty-one, Neil was greatly troubled with where the future of human space exploration was headed, especially in the United States. In a rare public appearance, he gave a speech to the Committee on Science, Space, and Technology of the House of Representatives, where he pointed to a lack of money and direction in the program, as well as a need for more imagination and creativity, as his areas of main concern.

Neil died on August 25, 2012, at the age of eighty-two. He used his last public appearances and interviews to speak about the work the United States and NASA had to do over the coming years to get back to the lunar surface. Yet, even with his concerns, he was confident that someday, before too long, people would again walk on the moon.

"I know one day, somebody is going to go fly back up there and pick up that camera I left," he said.

That, of course, begs the question . . .

Anyone feel up for a trip?

Just 480,000 miles to the moon and back again.

Timeline of Neil Armstrong's Life

1930 — Neil Armstrong is born on August 5 in Wapakoneta, Ohio

1932 — Neil Armstrong's father takes him to his first air show and his parents give him his first model plane

1937 — Goes on his first airplane flight

1938 — Attempts, and fails, to climb the tree in his backyard

1946 — Earns his pilot's license

1947 — Graduates high school; witnesses the plane crash; begins attending Purdue University

1949 — Reports for military duty

1955 — Graduates from Purdue

1956 — Marries Janet Shearon

1962 — Neil is selected for the second group of NASA astronauts

1966 — Commands Gemini 8 mission

1969 — Completes Apollo 11 mission; receives Presidential Medal of Freedom

1971 — Leaves NASA to teach at the University of Cincinnati

1994 — Neil and Janet are divorced

— Marries Carol Held Knight

2011 — Receives Congressional Gold Medal

2012 — Dies on August 25 at eighty-two years old

Bibliography

*Books for young readers

"Apollo 11: Technical Air-to-Ground Voice Transcription." Apollo Lunar Surface Journal. https://history.nasa.gov/alsj/a11/a11transcript_tec.html.

Armstrong, Neil, Edwin Aldrin, and Michael Collins. "Man walks on another world." *National Geographic*, December 1969, 738–749.

Barbree, Jay. *Neil Armstrong: A Life of Flight*. New York: Thomas Dunne Books, 2014.

*Edwards, Roberta. *Who Was Neil Armstrong?* New York: Penguin Workshop, 2008.

Engle, Michael. *Landing Eagle: Inside the Cockpit During the First Moon Landing*. Dublin, Ohio: Telemachus Press, 2019.

Fairhead, D., dir. *Armstrong*. 2019. United States/UK: Tin Goose Films, Haviland Digital, Mark Stewart Productions, Hays Films.

Hansen, James R. *First Man: The Life of Neil A. Armstrong*. New York: Simon & Schuster, 2005.

*Howard, Martin. *The Extraordinary Life of Neil Armstrong*. London: Puffin Books, 2019.

Parry, Dan. *Moonshot: The Inside Story of Mankind's Greatest Adventure*. London: Ebury Press, 2009.

*Weakland, Mark. *When Neil Armstrong Built a Wind Tunnel*. North Mankato, MN: Picture Window Books, 2018.

Weaver, Kenneth. "The flight of Apollo 11: 'One giant leap for mankind.'" *National Geographic*, December 1969, 752–787.